STEPPING-STONES

FOLLOWING A PATHWAY TO THE END OF LIFE

ELLIE ATHERTON

Stepping-Stones~Following a Pathway to the End of Life

Copyright © 2020 by Ellie Atherton

All rights reserved.

For information email ellie@eleanoratherton.com

Or visit https://eleanoratherton.com/

Library of Congress Control Number: 2020916084

ISBN 978-1-7354733-4-5 (paperback, first edition)

ISBN 978-1-7354733-1-4 (ebook, first edition)

Second paperback printing 2021

Printed in the United States of America.

Published by 3 Blessings Publications

Candia, N.H. 03034

Cover design by Ellie Atherton

Special thanks to my daughter for the original book cover art.

Laura Zorawowicz: Watercolor- *Beach Rocks~Sunrise*

No part of this book may be reproduced in any form or by any electronic or mechanical means, including information storage and retrieval systems, without written permission from the author, except for the use of brief quotations in a book review.

This is a work of creative nonfiction. All of the events in this memoir are true to the best of the author's memory. Some names and identifying features have been changed to protect the identity of certain parties. The author in no way represents any company, corporation, or brand mentioned herein. The views expressed in this memoir are solely those of the author.

ABOUT THE AUTHOR

Ellie Atherton has always had a love of writing and kept journals and diaries from a young age. She often wrote poetry for friends and family, and as a teen aspired to be both a writer and a teacher. She is an herbalist of more than forty years and a registered nurse of almost two decades. Stepping-Stones is her first published work. Ellie continues to provide support to patients and families as a private nurse advocate. She lives in New Hampshire, has three grown children, and three grandchildren.

DEDICATION

I lovingly dedicate this book to my three children Laura, Daniel, and Adam. You were my very first audience as I recounted these stories with amazement and wonder as they were unfolding. You listened with curiosity and openness, and when I was feeling sad, you compassionately offered me a healing hug. I appreciated always having you cheering me on and loving me through any heartbreak that came with my work of caring for the dying. Thank you for inspiring me to be the best teacher for you as I strived to learn and grow in my roles as a mom, nurse, herbalist, and ever-evolving human being. I love you with all my heart, and I am proud to be called your mother.

May the next generation, your children, my grandchildren Brennan, Calla, and Quinn, (hopefully more to come) be blessed with greater wisdom and acceptance of death like the generations of long ago. I look forward to all we will learn together from them, our wise little owls.

*In precious memory of my dear friend and mentor,
Wesley E. Burwell*

ACKNOWLEDGMENTS

First and foremost, the patients who were teaching me as they made their way through the final chapter of their lives were the book's inspiration. I could fill pages with the names of all the colleagues I worked with over the years whose guidance, presence, and knowledge made me a better hospice nurse. I fear I would leave someone out and dare not try. I feel it's best to thank one and all, for just as each puzzle piece is important, so were you in my journey to becoming a hospice nurse.

As a hospice director, I was privileged to have an incredible group of professionals on my team. Much of the work we did together is among the most impressive, compassionate work I have ever been a part of or witnessed. Though the days were long and the challenges were many, I will always feel proud of what we accomplished and all that I learned. Thank you for working in a way that meant putting your heart and soul into the work you did each day—for the benefit of our patients and their families.

My mom, Jane Dutcher, acted as my first run editor when the stories were still a tangled mess and straight from my heart. I am grateful for the way in which it connected us more deeply.

Barbara Rosner offered her eagle eye in the grammatical editor's role when the stories were in the first rough draft. This cleaner version she provided allowed me to see the stories in a new light and made my work of enhancing them more manageable. Barbara, I thank you from the bottom of my heart.

After writing all the stories, I decided to ask a varied group of people to read them to determine if there was any interest in the subject matter. I asked this group to read the stories while still in their roughest form, before embarking on a major editing process. All of their feedback helped me dramatically improve on the original book. The group was asked to provide details on how each story and its characters affected them.

Don Rosner was part of this group that I called my sample readers group. Don's honest, lengthy, and thorough responses far surpassed any other reader in the group. Don helped me shape the book by openly discussing the emotions and thoughts the stories were evoking in him. He encouraged me to give more detail to the stories by sharing more of my thoughts and feelings as the nurse and narrator. This change pulled the content from its original state of simplicity into a more evolved presentation. Don, I couldn't have done it without you.

My long time friend, Priscilla Drouin, helped me improve my writing craft and enhance my writer's voice. She taught me the power of using strong verbs over adjectives and adverbs. She also encouraged me to be more vulnerable when sharing my thoughts and feelings in the stories. Priscilla, I appreciated the opportunity to learn from you and will forever be grateful for our friendship.

With profound gratitude to the Burwell family for asking me into such a sacred time and for their input and written permission to share their story.

Finally, my professional editor, Beverly Ehrman, brought me to another level of writing and editing. She helped me to bring nuance and flow to the stories with insightful suggestions. Her guidance and mentoring allowed me to grow in awareness of the essential aspects of being a writer and reading the words from my readers' perspective. I am so proud of what we accomplished together, and I look forward to our future collaboration.

PREFACE

I began caring for the dying as an herbalist in the early '90s. A decade later, in 2003, I became a registered nurse, choosing hospice as the medical specialty that best fit me. My hospice nursing practice revolved around patient autonomy, and although this could present challenges, I discovered that nothing made patients happier than doing things their way. Once they had been informed of their medical options, I believed it was my job to support their choices, maintain their comfort, and walk beside them every step of the way.

My greatest teachers were the patients, and I came to refer to them as *the experts*. I was moved by their experiences, humbled by their unselfish ways in the face of death, and enlightened by what they shared with me.

In 2017, after more than twenty years of working in the capacity of a midwife to the dying, and many failed attempts to start writing this book, the words finally began to flow. I have written this book to honor *all* the patients I cared for and their ability to do things their way—patient autonomy. I also wrote the book for you, my readers, and listeners hoping it will allow you to discover more about death, reduce fears you may have around dying, and encourage you to live life more fully by following your own true path.

As I read through my journals and returned to each patient's situation, it was quite emotional for me. I was reminded of how much I loved all of these great people, and how privileged I was to be their nurse and support them in their journey out of this place we call life. I also spent a tremendous amount of time in meditation and quiet reflection as I worked to let go of some of the difficult situations I had faced while caring for them. Writing the stories was cathartic and necessary for me to move into the next chapter of my own life.

While writing the book, I continued discovering new and fascinating aspects of dying. The stories were still affecting me and changing me—even decades later. Maybe learning and growing in my own life during the book's hibernation led to my new discoveries. I'm not sure. All I know is that going back into the end-of-life situations with my patients and their families was awakening something inside me.

By definition, death means the end of something, the passing of something—we all experience loss in our everyday lives. As we enter our adult lives, we mourn the loss of carefree childhood days when playing was our purpose. We miss being part of a group or sports team. We reminisce about our teenage loves and adventures and recall family rituals no longer celebrated as distance separates us from one another. We mourn the end of a marriage, or the loss of a job we enjoyed. These are all deaths, by definition.

We don't generally consider these losses a death, but they are an endpoint. Nonetheless, the relationship or experience will remain a part of us.

In my first week as a hospice nurse, I met someone who would help me discover more about myself than any person in my life had before him—I called him my friend, my teacher, my

Gandhi. On a beautiful May afternoon, after sitting all day in orientation training, I was asked to participate in an outdoor meditation. As we made our meditative walk around the labyrinth, the leader spoke to us, saying, *Death is an inevitable part of life. As aspects of our lives or ourselves die, we are provided an opportunity for new pieces of life and self to be born.* The message resonated with me. It was the first of many lessons I would learn from this wise man.

Some food for thought before you begin reading the stories. The message of the Stepping-Stone Pathway came to me intuitively one day, and this quote is my explanation of it to one of my patients:

"In my symbolic example, you are walking on a path of stepping-stones as you approach the end of life. Each stone has a purpose. As you stand on each stone, you review the purpose and the memory it represents. You don't move forward to the next stone until you are ready for the next lesson or memory. Sometimes people step forward and then backward briefly. Eventually, and at their own pace, they walk forward on the path of stepping-stones."

May the stories from my teachers, the experts who walked the pathway to their death, help you accept the deaths in your own life and understand more about the one thing every human will face and succeed at—dying.

CONTENTS

Introduction	xix
1. Terms	1
2. COVID-19	3
3. Return to Dust	5
4. Ducks	12
5. Packing for the Journey	17
6. In an Orderly Fashion	28
7. The Gift of Giving	38
8. Forever on the Farm	45
9. Sail On	62
10. Her Way	75
11. The Matriarch	106
12. The Long Goodbye	133
Discussion Questions	195
What's next?	197

INTRODUCTION

Meeting people during some of the most private and emotional times of their lives is a huge privilege. Hospice was never simply a paycheck or just a job for me; it was a vocation.

I have been honored with a trust to guide patients and families along a sacred walk to a place I know exists but have not seen. I am thankful for having had the clear eyes and open mind needed to learn about its mysteries and discover the Stepping-Stones pathway. I have been given profound answers to patients' questions and continue to be amazed at how they came to me in perfect step with the circumstance.

I carry many lifetime secrets patients needed to release before finding the self-forgiveness necessary to leave this Earthly plane. I have heard countless patients speak of seeing deceased loved ones and comforting people at their bedside. I trust it is real. These patients had different religions, spiritual beliefs, and diseases, and were receiving different medications. I cannot accept the scientific theory that they were merely dehydrated, causing them to have similar dreams.

Having an awareness of the dying circumstance was enlightening. It allowed me to watch the process, the actual walk to death, each time, reinforcing the idea that the pathway awaits and opens for all of us. I often told patients we were going from one love to the next love—a love we are all deserving of.

Though this book is not about tragic sudden death or suicide, some lessons about dying may still apply; you should be the one to decide. It is also not about any one religious belief or doctrine. The patients in these stories all knew they were dying, and their unique stories show how each used their final days, weeks, or months to prepare to say goodbye to this life, and those they loved, in thoughtful and meaningful ways.

Readers may see similarities to their own experiences of caring for the dying. For example, many patients come home with chest tubes, require medications for breathing, have family caregivers who struggle with letting them go, and so on. After a death of a loved one, I frequently heard stories from caregivers of lights flickering, visions, or unusual events that indicated to the family that their loved one was all right. Any similarities you encounter in these stories must be considered merely a coincidence.

I hope a front-row seat with a compassionate view of how each person handles death differently helps you realize you have more control over the process than you thought possible. May it reduce fears about dying and better prepare you for your own death. You will choose how the stories affect you. I thank you for having the curiosity and courage to read on.

1

TERMS

If you need hospice services for yourself or a loved one, it will open a new world of terminology for you. I do use some of these terms in my book but did my best to minimize medical jargon. There are terms that you will see repeated throughout the book and I would like to offer some clarity before you begin reading.

Life review can begin months or weeks before a person dies. It refers to the way patients look back over their lifetime, remembering people, places, and events that had an impact on them. Patients will either discuss the memory or choose to keep it to themselves. Many patients referred to these thoughts as a dream, while others recounted them out loud as if they had just happened. Caregivers should not try to reorient the patients back to the present or tell them these thoughts are not real. Instead, ask them questions and encourage them to share more. This will help them move forward with less burden. Life review is an important part of the work patients must do before dying.

I often discuss **phlegm** in the throat, also known as terminal secretions. You may have heard some call this sound the death rattle; I never liked this term, and so I don't use it in the stories.

Basically, the phlegm accumulates as patients relax into their final days and the chest muscles no longer push the natural secretions around. In essence, this state of relaxation is what causes phlegm to accumulate in the upper airway. Patients are often less bothered by this phlegm and the sound it produces than the people who have to listen to it. Medications are used to dry up the phlegm, but sometimes it is not possible. Diseases that cause inflammation like cardiac disease, lung disease, and cancer often make for greater end-of-life secretions. Regardless, patients do not choke or suffocate and die from the secretions. Placing patients in a side-lying position, or head-elevated position, can provide for increased drainage and comfort.

Dying process refers to the phase when patients have stopped talking and are busy preparing to leave their physical body. At this stage they have what I called a *looking through you, not at you* effect to their eyes. They are often reaching their arms out and talking quietly to others we cannot see. It is best not to interrupt this work. You may sit at their bedside and watch in amazement at how long they can hold their weak arms above their bodies. Try lying flat for two minutes with your arms stretched toward the ceiling; it's hard work. It is a mystery, how in their weakened state, they have the strength to do this at length, sometimes for hours.

If you try to interact with them, they may ignore you, or speak to you briefly then return to their other conversation. I often thought it seemed like patients were watching a captivating movie being played on the ceiling, one that often caused patients to interact, laugh, and cry. When they finish with this interaction, their eyes become clear again and they will look at you as if you just arrived in the room.

Whenever possible, I tried to help families see the beauty and wonder of the process.

2

COVID-19

COVID-19 began to sweep through our world in early 2020, taking the lives of friends, neighbors, and loved ones. Unlike the patients in this book, many COVID-19 patients were not afforded time for end-of-life conversations, forgiveness, thank yous, and goodbyes. The lasting effects of departing this world in such a way linger with family and friends who loved them and those who did not know them but cared for them. Not having the opportunity to memorialize and bury loved ones has complicated this grief for countless families and communities.

I wish I could offer words that would mend your broken hearts, release your sadness, pain, and regrets, and reconnect you to the love of those you have lost. Please don't isolate yourself in your grief. Reach out to and lean on others who understand your suffering and strive to build a lasting bridge of strength and healing with them. Together we will learn how to heal from the tragedies of COVID-19. It will be a long road. I pray the efforts of love and compassion that we are witnessing around the world will spill over and make humanity kinder than ever before.

I would like to share this lesson I learned from the dying in hopes that it may offer you some small measure of comfort. The majority of the dying patients I cared for were much more concerned about their loved ones than for themselves. They told me they didn't want their death to destroy the goodness in others' lives or stop them from living fully. They wanted those they left behind to appreciate and live out their lives as happily and joyfully as possible. Of course, they knew their family and friends would grieve for them, but ultimately, they wanted them to find the strength to go forward in life without them. They said this was the best way to honor them and the life they had lived and shared.

My patients have taught me that all humans have an innate wisdom about death—even patients who are afraid or unprepared to die possess this knowledge. I believe the unseen dimensions of this wisdom are present and, at the end of every life, usher us out of this world. This statement is not linked to a specific doctrine or spiritual practice; instead, it is a lesson from the only real experts on death—the dying. It is based on observations and conversations with more than a thousand dying people of varied ethnicities, socioeconomic backgrounds, and belief systems.

These patients taught me that the intelligence of the human spirit, our innate wisdom, is something we should revere, draw strength from, and learn to trust; these unseen pieces of ourselves are the essential conduit during life and death. I was comforted to discover many dying patients could see someone in the room or had been visited by someone in a dream who had answers to their questions about dying and offered to walk with them.

3

RETURN TO DUST

My father-in-law, Fran, had an Aunt Beryl who was nine years old when he was born. They lived in the same New England-style house growing up—he and his parents in the upper-level apartment and his grandparents and aunt in the lower section of the home. Fran and Beryl were much like brother and sister in those early years. Beryl carried Fran around when he was a baby, then pushed him in the stroller when he was a toddler. She called him her "little doll." They remained close as adults and lived only about a mile apart for more than fifty years.

Fran was a kind man, and he and my mother-in-law remained welcoming to me after his son and I divorced. During my marriage, they often traveled to New Hampshire to spend weekends with us and usually joined us for a few days on our annual summer vacations to Cape Cod and Lake Sunapee. They were happy and easygoing guests. I have many great memories of the times we shared and the fun my family and I had with them. I am thankful I was able to enjoy a loving relationship with my in-laws until their deaths.

Like Fran, Aunt Beryl was not a churchgoer and did not speak of a connection to any faith. Fran called himself a *home Baptist* and once told me he believed that all humans go back to dust when they die.

Fran, at eighty-one, was at the end of his life and receiving hospice services at home. Aunt Beryl, at ninety, had experienced no major health issues throughout most of her long life. She was a widow who had been living in an apartment on her own for more than thirty years. She was active and social, often going out with friends for lunch and shopping. Although she developed macular degeneration in her mid-eighties, it didn't seem to slow her down at all. She had remarkable fortitude and rarely complained.

On the weekend that Fran was dying, the family called Aunt Beryl to see if she wanted to say goodbye to Fran in person. She was no longer driving due to her legal blindness and she and Fran were now living about thirty minutes apart. They would offer to drive her to Fran's home.

They tried calling her on Friday night but there was no answer. Since she was quite active, they assumed she was socializing at a neighbor's apartment. On Saturday they tried her a couple of times, and still no answer. Again, they thought she might be shopping or having dinner with friends, her usual activities. On Sunday morning when she didn't pick up, they became concerned and drove to her apartment to check on her.

When they arrived, she didn't answer the door. The apartment manager was able to unlock the door and let them in. Aunt Beryl was found barely conscious, lying on the floor next to the bed with a possible broken neck. She was weak, yet responsive. She had fallen on Friday night while attempting to put on her pajamas. Unfortunately, her med-alert button was on her bedside table and she could not reach it from the floor. She was in too much pain to move and tried yelling for help, but none of the neighbors heard her cries. She had been lying on the cold floor for more than thirty-six hours.

An ambulance transported her to the hospital in Keene, where they explained her injuries to her nephew. The emergency room staff reported to him and Beryl that there was nothing they could do for her broken neck, other than try to manage the pain. They told her nephew privately that she was likely to die within a couple of days. The plan was to transport her to Mary Hitchcock Hospital in Lebanon, New Hampshire, where she would receive comfort measures until she passed away.

Shortly after arriving at the hospital in Keene, Aunt Beryl began asking for me. She and I had remained very close, and of course, she knew I was a hospice nurse. The call came from the hospital to share the sad news and let me know she was requesting my presence. I had just returned from a week-long vacation in Aruba the night before and was propelled back to reality in an instant. My heart sank at the thought of the pain she had endured over those long hours on the floor and how shaken she must be from the whole ordeal.

I quickly decided to spend the final days of Aunt Beryl's life at her bedside in the hospital. My children learned from their dad, of Aunt Beryl's impending death and all three were saddened by the news. She held a special place in all of their hearts. My eldest son Dan was living in Utah with his young family and said he was so happy to think they had just visited in the fall and spent time with Aunt Beryl. My younger son Adam thought about making the trip, to say goodbye, but decided he wanted to remember her as the lively aunt he had always known. I agreed this was a mature decision. My daughter, Laura, at twenty-seven, chose to travel with me and stay with Aunt Beryl for those final days. Laura had never been with anyone who was dying but had been hearing stories about my patients for more than ten years so had some idea of what she was about to witness.

I worried aloud on our seemingly endless car ride through the mountains of New Hampshire about what condition we would find Aunt Beryl in. My years of pain management training and hands-on experience helped me to consider the worst. I knew we might have to offer sedation as an option to relieve the unrelenting pain of a broken neck. I wondered if she would be delirious from days of lying on the floor and the ensuing dehydration. Would she even recognize us?

We talked of her incredible constitution at her age and laughed about her strong will. She was never one to mince words; my children and I had delighted in her brutal honestly over the years. Though we expected it, she was still able to shock us in conversations.

When Laura and I arrived at the hospital in Lebanon, we were amazed to find Aunt Beryl lucid and joyful. She had not been told that we were coming, and was surprised and thrilled to see us. She immediately asked about my vacation, which brought laughter from not only the family but the medical staff.

Aunt Beryl was quickly transferred from the emergency room to a private room upstairs. The young nurse conducted her assessment and then a licensed nursing assistant bathed her and dressed her in a clean hospital gown. There was a small recliner in the room for overnight guests, but since both Laura and I planned to stay until she died the nurse brought in a small cot.

Fran was well on his way in his dying process by this time on Sunday evening. Because Aunt Beryl was lucid and since no one had shared the news, I decided to tell her that Fran was in his final days. She knew how poorly he had been doing so she was not surprised by the news. She was, of course, sad to think about him dying.

"Oh, my Frannie. I love him so much," Aunt Beryl said.

"It seems the two of you will be leaving this world in very

close proximity to one another and somehow, that seems fitting, Aunt Beryl," I said.

"Well, I suppose it does." She smiled.

She talked a lot that night to Laura and me, reminiscing about family, with no mention of her fall and more than thirty-six hours on the floor. She had never been one to show weakness. I imagine this came from growing up in a large family and living a rugged country life. Early Monday morning she was in tremendous pain and did not speak much, other than moans that were hard for Laura and me to listen to. After several unanswered requests for increased pain medication dosing, the staff finally responded and got her comfortable around eleven —she spoke to us once again. She asked to see the photo on my phone of my eighteen-month-old grandson, Brennan, her great-great-great nephew. She had always adored him and just speaking of him gave her great joy. I had begun sending her photos of Brennan when he was born and continued to send them at each stage of development. Due to her macular degeneration, I had them enlarged to 5x7 or 8x10 so she could make out more details of his cute little face and frame. She always placed them under the glass on her coffee table, and said she enjoyed looking at them daily with her large magnifying glass.

"Oh, I just love this little boy," she exclaimed, as she looked at the photo of him in the outfit, she had sent for his first birthday. Being so young, Brennan will never remember the joy he brought Aunt Beryl in her final years, but I recount the stories to him often, hoping he will come to know how much she loved and adored him.

Around two in the afternoon, Aunt Beryl finally seemed at peace and began to relax into dying. Laura and I were grateful to see her turn this corner. Laura updated her dad via a text message and told him that she was more comfortable.

After this interaction on Monday afternoon, Aunt Beryl fell

into a deep sleep and did not speak to us again, offering only nods in response to our questions about her comfort. By late Monday evening, she hadn't spoken to us for more than ten hours. Laura and I were sleeping when, at eleven, she called out to Fran.

"Oh, Frannie, you're here? Oh, I love you, I love you," she said, clear as a bell, waking us from a sound sleep. Then she mumbled as she reached her arms straight up above her chest; we could not make out exactly what she was saying. Still, it was beautiful, and evoked a feeling of awe in both of us. Without speaking, Laura and I both knew what it meant. As quickly as she had begun speaking, Aunt Beryl stopped and returned to her deep sleep, as if her visitor had gone. Our thoughts were confirmed ten minutes later, when Laura received a text message from her father saying: *Grandpa Fran died a few minutes ago.*

I have goosebumps as I write this. Here were two people who had no religious beliefs. Each had maintained that they did not believe in God, heaven, or anything beyond this life. Yet they were somehow communicating with one another. One lay dying in Hanover, New Hampshire; the other in Bernardston, Massachusetts. If I had been asked to guess beforehand, I would have put money on Aunt Beryl going first to help her "little doll" Fran cross over. At some point their roles must have switched, and unbeknownst to us, Fran was now caring for her.

Laura and I cried as we consoled each other, thinking of the loneliness of his widow—my mother-in-law, Laura's grandmother—a woman we both cherished. Finally, around one in the morning, we fell back to sleep. The night remained quiet as our fearless woman worked her way toward Fran.

Aunt Beryl, after speaking to Fran, never spoke again. Time passed slowly Tuesday morning as her breathing became labored and rapid, with intermittent breaks. When her pain spiked her morphine pump settings were increased, with fewer requests than the day before—small blessings. I frequently replaced the cool washcloth on her forehead as she perspired and brought in shallow rapid breaths throughout her marathon. At last her breathing slowed as she crossed the finish line. She died peacefully in the early afternoon as Laura and I watched her gently push out her last breath of life.

4

DUCKS

Though I had only met this sweet Italian gentleman a few times, he seemed like an old friend. Vinny was small in stature, and always dressed in a way that suggested old-school classiness to me. I enjoyed being in the presence of his positive attitude and gentle nature.

After Vinny's wife died, his house became much too quiet. He missed her company and their relaxed way together. Often, while cooking their favorite Italian dishes, they would delight in a glass of wine as the meal simmered to perfection. Since her death, his days had become suspended in an unwelcome drawn-out fashion.

In an attempt to raise his spirits, he began venturing down the hill near his home, to the beautiful pond and its surroundings. He made an effort to gather pieces of bread, rolls, and seeds to feed to his feathered friends, the large family of ducks that lived in the pond. This daily ritual became one of his favorite pastimes.

Vinny had few visitors other than his daughter Flora who was an only child. She had been assisting her dad for years, commencing with the passing of her mom. She kept the small home neat as a pin, the way her mother had. Flora had a full-time job; on weekdays her visits were in the evenings, and this afforded them some time to enjoy a meal together. She cooked using her mom's family recipes, filling the home with the familiar aromas that soothed her dad's lonely heart. Weekend visits were longer, and Vinny looked forward to them. Although Flora focused on completing the housework first, their trips to the pond were highlights of the weekend for both of them.

I can still remember our first meeting and the way Vinny's blue eyes lit up as he told me about how the ducks swam to the shore and practically ate out of his hands. He had remarked that these beautiful creatures brought joy back into his life, and he looked forward to his daily visits with them. He said when the ducks would see him approaching, they would quack and swim in circles as if playing Ring Around the Rosie. Apparently, the duck family enjoyed Vinny's visits as well.

In the years after his wife's passing, Vinny continued his uplifting practice of feeding the ducks from spring to late fall. He said he often wondered if the same group was returning each year or if some had died and their young had upheld the tradition. Either way, he was excited about spring's arrival after long winter months of doing puzzles and watching too much television.

As Vinny became more debilitated, walking even short distances was a taxing effort and, because of this, his daily visits with his feathered friends dwindled. The happiness he had felt while spending time with his duck family was hard to replace. In an effort to stave off yet another significant loss in his life, Vinny pushed himself to maintain at least a few visits each week. Once back home, he was exhausted but glad he had made the effort. After lunch he would settle into his recliner on the sunporch, his favorite place to be, for a short nap.

Sadly, within a few weeks, Vinny was too feeble to make the trip down the hill and back up again. On the afternoon I visited, his daughter Flora greeted me at the door saying her dad was waiting for me on the sunporch and had a story to share.

Flora beamed. "You know how my dad loves to feed the ducks, right?"

"Yes, I remember."

"He's too weak to walk up and down the hill now."

"I heard he was no longer able to make the trip. I'm sorry." I felt sadness knowing how much Vinny had enjoyed feeding and spending time with the ducks.

"Well, that's what we have to tell you. You won't believe this!" Flora exclaimed with a twinkle in her own blue eyes, much like the one I had seen in her dad's when he spoke of the ducks.

"Let's go out to the sunporch to sit with my dad. He's eager to tell you the story."

I followed Flora down a narrow hallway, walls adorned with photos of Vinny, his wife, and Flora, until we reached the sunporch with its beautiful view of a private nature preserve. The sun shone through the large windows surrounding the room on three sides, warming the bright and cozy space. In the backyard, a large post with several bird feeders graciously offered sustenance to more of Vinny's feathered friends.

There I found my Italian gentleman sitting in his recliner, looking out the window at the birds as they savored their meal. Vinny looked up as we entered.

"Hello," he said, looking a bit worn and not as cheerful as usual.

"I hear you have a story for me today."

"Yes, have a seat, please. You're going to love this."

I set my things down and got comfortable in the chair next to him, curious to hear what he had to share with me. Vinny had a great smile and the sweetest demeanor. There was something special about this man, and I always looked forward to visiting because he had a way of filling me with joy.

Vinny started telling his story. "Unfortunately, I'm too weak to walk down and feed my ducks every day," he said. Vinny looked out the window, lost in his memories.

"I'm sorry, Vinny. I remember how much you loved seeing your ducks every day." Much to my surprise, he laughed.

"Well, I guess they must have missed me too," he said, turning back to face me.

I watched his usual cheerful energy returning as he continued telling his story.

"The other day, Flora came running in here, yelling that the ducks were coming up the driveway."

"What?" I said in astonishment. "You've got to be kidding!"

"No, I'm not. Those silly ducks waddled all the way around my house."

I was intrigued by the unusual activity of the ducks and eager to hear the rest of the story.

"They went right by the windows here." He pointed to the windows facing the backyard. "We watched them as they went marching by, one by one, in a neat row."

"It was amazing!" Flora added, unable to contain her excitement any longer. "And every single one looked up as they went by. I swear it."

Vinny confirmed the extraordinary detail. "It's true. Then they continued around the house and headed back down the hill to the pond. It was incredible!" He clapped his hands and laughed again.

"And what I can't figure out, is how they knew where I lived." Vinny paused, giving me a curious look. "My house and driveway aren't visible from the pond. You may not be aware, but you have to go down the hill and to the right to get to the pond. There's no way they could have seen my house from that vantage point. How did they find me?"

The three of us sat in silent wonderment, pondering the question. After a few moments I said, "What a wonderful story, Vinny. When I write my book, may I include your story?"

Vinny didn't hesitate. "Of course you can." Then he shifted his body and turned to me, looking directly into my eyes, and asked, "What do you suppose the visit means?"

Pleased that he had asked for my opinion, I replied, "Oh my gosh, there's only one thing it could mean! They came to say goodbye to you and thank you for feeding them and being their friend over the years."

He smiled at me. "Do you think so?"

"They searched you out, didn't they? They made an effort to find you—to give you a message. I believe finding you was important to them. They gave you a farewell parade, Vinny!"

This humble man, a bit teary-eyed now, said, "You could be right. You know in all the years I've lived here I have never once seen the ducks venture up that road."

"I guess seeing you again made a great adventure worthwhile. Isn't that amazing? I suppose animals are wiser than we give them credit for." I winked at him.

"Could be. Thanks for listening to my story," Vinny said, patting my arm.

A few weeks later, my bird-loving friend died peacefully with the care and comfort of his lovely daughter by his side.

I will never forget the powerful message about the intuition animals possess. In the coming years, I would learn more from a great mentor of mine about this intriguing phenomenon, and as I raised my awareness, my own life was enhanced.

All humans are born with this innate intuition, though I have come to believe it is overlooked or forgotten by most. Even when we have chosen to be distant from it, the instinct hibernates within, until we are hungry enough to open ourselves up to the wisdom.

5

PACKING FOR THE JOURNEY

I met Helen quite a few times during my hospice training, when I shadowed a long-time hospice nurse colleague. Helen was a little spitfire, all of maybe four foot six inches tall when she stood up straight, which she rarely did because leaning forward helped her breathe more easily. She was a widow who lived alone in a quaint one-bedroom apartment in the country. It had everything she needed: a galley kitchen, an open-concept dining/living room area, and a small bedroom. The close proximity of the rooms was a gift because any movement caused Helen to experience labored breathing, even with her continuous use of oxygen.

Helen had no children and no local family to act as caregivers when the need arose. She did have a sweet neighbor who lived directly across the hall from her. Claire had been checking on Helen for years and helped her by delivering groceries and attending medical visits. As Helen declined, Claire began checking on her each morning and evening.

Over the summer months, when my colleague had time off, I would be the one to make the visits on my own. I grew to love this independent woman. I always told her she was as *cute as a button*. She would smile, laugh, and shake her hand at me.

"Never mind," she would say.

I sensed that she appreciated the compliment but felt uncomfortable accepting it. This reaction seemed right in line with her tough exterior. I wasn't buying it, though. There was a sweetness underneath her well-polished armor.

One day, just as I was leaving, Helen asked if she could give me something. Her late husband had collected butterflies, and she said she wanted me to have one of the preserved and delicately framed insects as a remembrance of her. Since we had only met a few times, this gesture took me by surprise; her thoughtfulness touched me deeply.

On more than one occasion in my life, I had experienced a butterfly landing on my hand, allowing me to admire it for a few moments before it flew off again. I had a heart for the stunning winged creatures.

I gratefully accepted Helen's gift of kindness, admiring the colorful wings of the butterfly she had chosen for me. I gave her a hug and thanked her for the generous and meaningful gift. I was elated by her kindness—it represented her trust and acceptance of me.

As our relationship grew, I worried about who would care for Helen when she was too weak to care for herself. At weekly meetings of the hospice team, we often talked about what would happen to Helen. We hadn't determined who would stay with her in those final days. Of course, we had no way of knowing how long she would be bedbound and need assistance. This variable made it challenging to find caregivers who were able to commit to an open-ended role.

These questions regarding her care remained unanswered because Helen didn't want to discuss them during our visits, always waving them off and changing the subject. Her reaction made it even more difficult for hospice staff to help her formulate a realistic plan. She kept saying she would figure it out.

I worried about how Helen would manage to medicate herself if she was having trouble breathing and was too weak to get to her medication. I also worried about her falling, in her weakened state, and breaking a hip. That scenario usually ended in a hospital or nursing home death and I knew that would surely add to her baseline anxiety level. It was sad to think that Helen might be alone at the end of her life.

When the hospice staff embarked on conversations around her care, they did evoke emotion in Helen. On several occasions, she told me that she was annoyed with God.

"He's making me wait too long. I've been ready to die for such a long time, and I have prayed and prayed for God to take me. I can't understand why He hasn't yet."

I stayed silent as she vented her anger at God, and I had to wonder what was holding her intrepid spirit back. The next time my colleague went on vacation, I was assigned to visit Helen. I decided that if she started the same conversation, I was going to ask her what she thought might be stopping her from getting her wish to die. On that afternoon, after I had finished her assessment, she asked me again why God was taking so long.

"I don't have the answer to that. I think you probably do, though," I responded as I had planned.

"What do you mean by that answer?" Helen was clearly perturbed with me. "I would have died months ago if I knew!" she said, exasperated.

"Well, let's talk about this. Are you worried about anything? Is there something you're afraid of?" I asked her as I stared back at the daggers she was throwing me.

She became defensive. "Do you mean, am I afraid of dying?"

"Yes, that's precisely, what I mean," I said.

"Well, I do worry about gasping for breath at the end of my

life," she admitted, letting some of the anger fall away as the truth tumbled out.

"That's what the liquid morphine is used for," I told her. "These syringes will always be at your bedside and next to your recliner, in case you need them." I showed her one of the one-milliliter syringes that held just under a quarter of a teaspoon when filled to the brim. "You've been telling us that the morphine helps you breathe easier."

"Yes, I notice that I won't huff and puff when I walk if I take one syringe beforehand."

"We'll just have to make sure we have a caregiver here with you when you're unable to give them to yourself," I said, opening Pandora's box again. I knew this was another opportunity to figure out who was going to be with her when she was dying. Helen said nothing.

I went on. "Who could administer the medication to make sure your breathing stays comfortable? Who do you think your end-of-life caregiver could be, Helen?" I asked, hoping at last for the answer to this looming question.

"I think my neighbor, Claire, would come. She's wonderful. She'll be here for me," she said with conviction.

"Is it okay for me to call and check with Claire today?" I asked, not wanting to let the long-awaited opportunity slip past.

"Yes, you can call her."

"Okay, great. Let's call her in a few minutes after we finish your assessment. Is there anything else you worry about when it comes to dying?"

She had a far-off look in her eyes as she thought about the question. After a minute, I smiled and said, "Can I ask you ... Helen, have you had a good life?"

"Oh, my dear, I've had a tough life!" she said, pushing out all the air her worn-out lungs could offer. I felt the pain and effort of it, like a knife. My heart sank. Though I had asked for it, this truth was not what I had expected. Wanting to honor the privilege of the moment with such a private woman, I leaned toward her to listen.

"My parents abused me when I was a child. When they were old, frail, and dying, I cared for both of them." Her shoulders sagged as the words came out. I understood the daunting task it must have been for her—physically and emotionally.

"That was an amazing gift to give them, in light of what they gave you," I said, hoping to extend compassion and possibly a tiny bit of healing by validating Helen's selfless sacrifice.

"Well, my husband and I agreed it was the right thing to do. I'm still glad I did it. Somehow it felt good at the time. But honestly, now I'm afraid to see them again," Helen said, looking down at her lap as if confessing a sin.

It was so unsettling for me to think of this petite, fragile woman still suffering from their abuse after her parents were dead and fearing they could abuse her again in the afterlife. How horrible! I knew the best answer was inside her own precious heart and soul.

"Do you mean you're afraid to see your parents again in heaven?" I asked, hoping to clarify her fears.

"Yes, in heaven. My dad hurt me and messed with my mind. I was so afraid of him. I don't ever want to see him again."

I could see the fear in her eyes, like a scared child. This angst was not something I had seen before in this seemingly fearless woman.

"Helen, you've told me how strongly you believe in God and how you look forward to going to heaven to be with your husband. Do you believe that God would let your father hurt you again in heaven?"

She was silent for a minute, looking uneasy. I had to resist the urge to scoop her up and hug her as if she had been a lost child.

She broke the silence. "No, I don't think God would ever let anyone hurt me again."

Relieved to hear this response, I said, "Well, maybe that's part of what's holding you back."

I let the thought settle in. She was quiet and did not disagree. I reached for her hand, leaned in closer, and gazed into her fear-filled eyes. "May I make a suggestion?"

"Sure, dear. I would love to hear it," Helen said, worn out by the dredged-up fear running through her head and our brief, but intense, conversation.

I let my intuition speak, not knowing where the thought would lead me. "Helen, pack up all the good memories of your lifetime. The good memories of your husband, who you said was the most wonderful man in the world and made you feel special." I squeezed her hand to offer support to her and push back my tears. She nodded and looked at me with watery eyes and a touch of curiousness.

"I like the sound of that. I like that very much," she said with the fear no longer visible in her eyes. Her feeble body sat more upright; she grew in strength. "You're right. I don't need those bad memories anymore. They're over and done!" the feisty woman said as she pounded her tiny fist on the table, her spirit emerging right before my eyes.

"My husband was such a great man. I miss him so much and I can't wait to be with him again. Thank you, Ellie. I will pack up my good memories."

"Could you use a hug?"

"Absolutely, my dear."

I helped Helen stand up next to the kitchen table. She reached her arms around my waist and gave me a big squeeze. I would have responded with a big squeeze in return if not for fear of hurting her frail frame. So instead, I gently held on and let her determine the force and length of the hug. As quickly as the conversation started, it ended. When she finally let go, she said, "I'm going to sit down in my recliner and take off my oxygen so I can have a smoke."

"Okay," I said, not surprised by her need to move on from the emotional conversation. I knew trying to stop Helen from smoking was a useless exercise.

I set to work gathering up the syringes that were next to her recliner and on the small table by her bed, prefilling them with liquid morphine. Once the vital task was complete, I sat on the couch next to her recliner and began my nursing documentation. Just as I had finished and her cigarette was out, she put her oxygen back on. There came a knock at the door.

"Come in," Helen said in her raspy voice. Her neighbor, Claire, entered with a cheerful hello and a smile that lit up the room. I had met her once before and enjoyed her positive energy.

"Hello, my dear," Helen said. "So good to see you. Ellie and I have been having a great talk." I was surprised by her description of our discussion.

"Oh, is that right? About what?" the neighbor asked.

"You tell her." Helen motioned to me with an arthritic finger.

My privilege, I thought. Not just to tell Claire, but to have been trusted in the first place to have such an intimate conversation.

"Well, today, while we were talking, Helen said she was confused about why God hasn't come to take her yet."

The neighbor nodded and, with eyebrows raised, shot me a look; apparently, she had heard this too.

"I suggested that maybe she needed to pack her bags."

"Pack her bags?" Claire looked confused.

"Yes." I smiled at her perplexed look. "I meant it metaphorically. I suggested that she pack up only her good memories to take to heaven with her and leave any sad memories behind."

"Oh, that's lovely," Claire said, glancing at Helen, who was smiling and nodding in agreement.

"Thank you, but I can't take credit for it. It came to me as we were talking. I guess God was guiding me to help Helen with this dilemma today." I winked at them. We all laughed, and a sweet peace washed over the room. I had felt this before with some of my other patients and loved the deepness of it. I trusted that something greater than myself, greater than all of us, was at work.

"We also talked about who would care for her and stay with her as she becomes weaker and needs more help." I waited, holding my breath, hoping for Helen's wish to come true. The beautiful friend didn't hesitate.

"I've been checking on her often for a few days now. I come over once during the night and every morning, afternoon, and evening, and I don't mind staying here on the couch if I need to."

I was relieved to learn this and couldn't wait to leave a message on the nurses' line for the team to hear. Another divine intervention, I thought to myself.

"You're such a great neighbor and friend, Claire," Helen said to her angel friend.

"That's wonderful. Can I review the comfort kit medications with you? Do you have a minute now?" I asked, wanting to ensure Claire felt prepared for the physical changes that would arise in the coming days.

"I do have time, yes."

I headed toward the fridge to retrieve the comfort kit so we could review it together. Claire met me at the kitchen table. There were medications for fever, nausea and vomiting, anxiety, pain, shortness of breath, and a symptom referred to as terminal secretions. I prepared Claire for the breathing changes and phlegm that might accumulate in Helen's airway, explaining that both were expected changes at the end of life. I removed the blue booklet from the hospice folder, a fourteen-page well-written description of the physical signs I had described, so caregivers knew what to expect.

Claire saw me pull it out. "I already read through it a few weeks ago when the social worker visited. I found it interesting and helpful."

"Do you have any questions about anything you read?"

"No, but I've noticed many of the changes mentioned in the booklet."

"Is that good?" Helen asked.

"Oh yes. It means you are well on your way, Helen," I said, praising her efforts. Claire nodded in agreement.

I too had noticed many of the changes and could easily understand why Helen wondered why she was still here. But I also realized she would die when she was truly ready to die. I had seen fear hold many patients back, so I felt an incredible sense of relief for Helen. We had discovered the fear that held her back, how to overcome it, and found someone to care for her when she was dying—it seemed like we had hit the trifecta.

A few days later, no heavy burdens to hold her here, Helen got her long-awaited wish. It was in the early morning hours, and I was covering the overnight on-call shift. Her dear friend, Claire, informed me that Helen was gone. She said that she was so thankful she had spent the night.

"I'm glad you were there too. Are you okay?"

"Oh, I'm fine. What happens next?"

"I can be there in about twenty-minutes, and then after I pronounce her, I'll contact the funeral home for you."

"Okay, I'll see you soon. Thank you."

And she was gone; the phone buzzed in my ear. I felt privileged that I would be the one to perform the pronouncement.

When I arrived, Claire greeted me at the door with a hug. Then, with that beautiful smile, she shared this story.

"The last thing she said last night, after I got her settled into bed, was that she wanted me to help her pack. I told her I felt honored, remembering your conversation and the symbolism. She said all she needed to take with her were her good memories and thanked me for being her friend and helping her. We never really packed anything physically, of course. I simply listened as she recounted stories of the happy times and the love she and her husband had shared.

"Then she drifted off to sleep. I slept on the couch so I could be close. I got up a few times during the night to medicate her for rapid breathing. Soon afterward, she was pretty peaceful, so I went back to lie down on the couch to rest again. It was hard to sleep because I kept listening to her breathing and that quiet rumbling in her throat. The medicine helped with the phlegm after a few doses, and then the rumbling stopped. I think it was after that when I finally did fall asleep.

"I checked on her early in the morning. When I entered the bedroom I noticed she was still, and I didn't hear her breathing. That's when I realized that she had gone peacefully in her sleep."

"Oh, I'm so proud of Helen and happy that she is at peace. She did such a great job of facing her fears. Thank you, Claire. What a wonderful gift you gave to her by being here. She was able to die peacefully with a dear friend near, in the comfort of her own home. And thanks for helping her pack only her good memories," I said with a smile, still amazed that those words had come to me.

"I was happy to be here with her. I loved her like a mother,"

"Oh, that's so nice. You know, I like to tell caregivers that their generous gift of caregiving will ultimately come back to them again and again in their own lives."

"Knowing Helen as I did, and remembering her, will both be lasting gifts for me."

Together we washed Helen's body and dressed her in a pretty

outfit. She looked as lovely as ever, even in death. After the funeral director left with Helen, Claire and I hugged and said our goodbyes.

As I drove away in the quiet of the early morning hour, I thought again about my words—the suggestion that came to me intuitively about packing the good memories. I thought about the fact that I had never heard or said those words before to anyone. They seemed so incredibly fitting at the moment. Actually, they seemed appropriate for many of the dying people I had already met. Could it be that the message is fitting for all of us?

Since then, I have suggested packing good memories many times over. Patients who were struggling to lay distressing memories to rest reported that the symbolism helped them move forward. I was grateful I had listened to my intuition and was able to share the profound but simple message in a way that helped others.

I was moved by the words that had come to me, so a few days after Helen died I decided to meditate on them. I came away with this: When we embark on dying, we should gather all of the love and kindness granted to us during our lifetime, no matter how big or small, and pack it into our soul as sustenance in preparation for our journey. All of the pain, hardship, and suffering we endured can now be laid to rest— their lessons no longer necessary. These lessons are the stumbling blocks of life, the challenges we've encountered. At the end of life, their presence no longer serves us. At life's end, it is best to allow the heavy burdens to fall away from our path and let our joyful spirit guide us forward.

IN AN ORDERLY FASHION

*P*rior to my initial visit, I had reviewed Robert's medical history and knew he was in the last few months of his life. He said he and his family were well aware that once he stopped treatments his time left on Earth would be limited. He told me he planned to get his affairs in order, to the best of his ability, before leaving his loving family. At that time, I had no idea of the depth of his commitment.

I was surprised by his many questions; it felt almost like he was interrogating me. He wanted to know how long I had been a hospice nurse, and if I had cared for other patients with a similar diagnosis to his. He had great pointed questions, for sure, and I'll admit it was a bit intimidating at times—especially because I had been a hospice nurse for less than two years and still had so much to learn.

I had great respect for his questions and his need to know all the details. I understood he was attempting to build trust in me as a caregiver, knowing I would support not just him, but also his cherished family. After all, he was allowing me into one of the most important and intimate times of his life, and I never took such responsibilities lightly.

The admission was cordial and reasonably straightforward; Robert had done his homework with regard to his disease and the treatment options available to him. He had a clear understanding of how quickly he could die after stopping his treatments.

Robert was a man who wanted to ensure he had the right people on his team. He was not interested in visits from the social worker or the hospice chaplain, but he made a nice connection with a volunteer. He told me that he and Mike talked about politics in a lively and passionate way. Robert looked forward to Wednesday-afternoon visits with Mike.

Robert said he expected me to keep him informed of his options for medical care. He wanted me to understand that he would not be rushing into any decisions. Robert was a thinker and a planner, and he was not going to change now. This was how he managed throughout his life and continuing in this way was most comfortable for him. He often took notes during my visits, so I knew he would keep me on my toes. I had a feeling that I was about to learn some valuable lessons from this strong and thorough man. I made suggestions in order to improve his comfort and he always wanted to think about them before making a decision. I respected his wishes and we moved at his pace.

Robert tried his best to maintain as much independence in his daily routines as possible. He said the time he spent with family was precious, and he did everything in his power to be upbeat and positive when they were around.

After a month of visits, Robert began to share more with me about what he had on his checklist and considered necessary to accomplish prior to his death. As the patriarch, he had managed everything for the family. Recently, he had begun helping his wife understand how to take over some of those tasks. Most were related to financial matters and household maintenance decisions —jobs Rachel had never had to worry about before.

This situation is a common one in relationships; each person carries responsibilities that the other rarely needs to consider. Passing them off can be challenging and sometimes negatively affects the little time left for the couples to spend together. Still, the shift is a necessary one on several levels. The patient needs to know who will take over the tasks, while the person taking them over has to learn how to manage them.

The patients are generally worried that their loved ones will not be able to handle all of the tasks on their own. They are concerned the additional responsibilities will weigh heavily on those they leave behind. Sometimes, knowing others plan to step in and offer support can reduce this worry dramatically for the patient.

As Robert's remaining days became fewer, he appeared more relaxed during visits; the low-level anxiety I had previously noticed was gone and he had stopped talking about his unfinished business. As was my practice with all patients, I asked Robert if he was worried about any aspect of pain, transitioning, dying, or family. He told me he was not at all concerned about pain or transitioning. He said that his faith was strong, and he felt comfortable and confident that he would be at peace when it came time for him to die. He said making sure that everything was in order for his girls, as he called them, would grant him the most peace.

Robert had worked hard to get his affairs in order, and on this day, he told me everything was in place. I was a bit surprised to hear this. I had watched other people who were organized or controlling struggle at the end of life. Many became more anxious as they discovered they had created an unrealistically long to-do list and were unable to complete it before they died. I noticed these unfinished aspects of life placed a heavy burden on the patients. Sometimes this hindrance would make them restless in their final weeks and days of life. I had often observed this dilemma holding patients with one foot here on Earth and the other trying to step into the beyond. They just couldn't seem to do it, not very easily, anyway.

This was not the case with Robert. He was a determined, kind, and loving man. All his goals focused on making things better for the people who were so important to him. I rarely heard him speak of his struggles or discomfort. I was learning firsthand from Robert about the importance of completing unfinished business and how it allowed a sense of calm to enter.

On the day Robert said he had decided to stop his treatments, we all knew it wouldn't be long before he would have to leave his beloved family. My heart broke for him, imagining how he finally came to this somber place. His wife and only daughter stood by his decision. Robert was quite tired and weak, spending more time sleeping than awake most days. It had become evident to his wife and daughter that he was getting ready to say goodbye to them.

I had met his daughter Carrie on only one occasion, and found her to be a lovely, vibrant young woman. She had a great intellect like her dad, combined with the grace, beauty, and poise of her mom. Carrie pulled me aside and said she was thinking of spending the night with her parents. She thought she could be a support for her mom, allowing her to get some much-needed sleep, while she would be available for her dad if he needed anything. I told her I thought that was an excellent idea; sleep would be a nice gift for her mom, who had become weary in recent weeks as Robert's care had increased.

I was always amazed that caregivers had a Goliath-like strength and ability to provide care at all hours of the day and night and somehow carry on in this way—sometimes for weeks and months on end. The loss of consistent sleep, coupled with the difficulty of watching a loved one slowly slip away, takes its toll. Ask anyone who has been a caregiver in these situations. The deep exhaustion is hard to describe with words.

I reviewed the medications in the hospice comfort kit with Rachel and Carrie and wrote down the name of each medication, the symptom it was used for, and how often each one could be administered. I had learned previously from fatigued families that writing down the details is essential, especially during emotionally draining times. Caregivers have too many thoughts and feelings occupying their minds; we should never expect them to remember verbal medical instructions. I made a practice of providing a paper tracking sheet for caregivers to record the doses and times they gave the medications. This simple tool made the work easier for them, while also reducing their stress around giving the medications. Caregivers often worried about forgetting to give medicine or giving too much. Having written instructions reinforced that they were doing things right.

After the family's careful review of the tracking sheet and their confirmed understanding of it, I went in to check on Robert once more before leaving. He had been napping during the last part of my visit and was just waking. I updated him about what had transpired during the time I had spent with his wife and daughter, explaining that I had reviewed the comfort kit medications with them. I told him about the written instructions and the tracking sheet.

"That sounds helpful. I think this is all becoming a bit challenging for Rachel. Thank you for giving them ways to reduce the stress." Robert's voice was weak, but he managed a soft smile.

I thought he would appreciate the organizational aspect of our plan and was glad he felt it might give some relief to Rachel as well. He thanked me for taking more time with them on this longer-than-usual visit. I asked him if he was having pain, and he said he was not uncomfortable at all. I asked, as always, if he had any questions for me.

Robert didn't answer, which was unusual for him. Instead, he asked, "When will you be back?"

"I plan to visit you daily now, Robert, if that's acceptable."

"I would appreciate that, more for them than for me. Thank you."

"Of course. You're welcome, Robert. I hope you can get some rest tonight. Carrie is planning to stay so Rachel can get more rest too."

"That sounds perfect. Rachel has been amazing, and I so appreciate her."

"Yes, she's a good nurse, Robert. Don't fire that one," I said with a laugh and wink.

"Never," he said.

Robert was not a patient I ever hugged. I had asked, as I always did at my first visit, and he said he would much prefer a handshake, so that was our practice. It was more business-like, and I respected that this was more comfortable for him. This afternoon, I reached down toward the bed and squeezed his hand instead of shaking it.

"I'll see you tomorrow." I smiled at him, and he squeezed my hand, holding it longer than I would have expected. His version of a hug, I thought.

"Goodbye, Ellie, and thank you," he said as he patted and then rubbed the top of my hand. It was the simplest of hugs in my book; I was grateful for the more profound meaning it offered.

Knowing we were entering his final days, I had to explain what to do at the time of death before ending the visit. I told Rachel and Carrie that a nurse would come to perform the pronouncement once they called to inform us of his passing, and that we would also notify the funeral home.

"Take your time when he goes. There's never any rush to call hospice or remove him from home afterward. Do what seems right for you," I encouraged them.

Early the next morning, I received a call from the overnight on-call nurse saying that Robert had died, and his family wanted to wait for me to be back on duty to perform the pronouncement. I was not surprised by their request, knowing how private the family had always been, likely not wanting a stranger in their home during such a sacred time. I must admit, though, my initial reaction to the news of his death was surprise. Even though it was six a.m., I immediately called to let them know I could come when they felt ready. Carrie answered the phone.

"Carrie, it's Ellie. I'm so sorry."

"Thank you. We're doing okay."

"I can come out whenever you're ready."

"We remembered what you said, and we didn't call when my dad died around four; we called family instead and waited until six to call hospice. Relatives who live nearby arrived to say a final farewell to my dad and offer their love and support to us."

"Good for you," I said, praising their ability to take their time and privately mourn the loss with loved ones before calling hospice.

"Everyone who wanted to see him this morning has already come, and some are still here with us. But you can come anytime. Are you on duty already?"

"No, I start at eight, but I'm happy to head your way now if that's best for you. I would arrive around six forty-five."

"That would be great. Let me run it by my mom; please hold."

"Sure." I could hear the muffled conversation taking place, and she returned swiftly.

"Six forty-five would be fine. Thank you. We'll see you soon."

"You're welcome, Carrie. I'll see you in a bit."

On the way to the house to perform Robert's pronouncement, I thought about how strong, organized, and thoughtful he had been in his preparation for dying. I recalled that Robert had told me, just the week before, that he had everything in order. He had done precisely what he had outlined in our early visits and insisted he was going to do before he died. When he felt certain he had everything in order, as planned, he made his way out of this world.

Here was another important lesson for me about the strength and determination of the human spirit. I loved that I was able to pay attention and learn from Robert. So why was I surprised when I learned he had died? It was because Robert was alert and lucid twelve hours prior to his death, and this was unusual. Most patients took several days to settle into a peaceful place before dying—I suppose that speaks to his resoluteness.

Rachel greeted me at the door, teary-eyed, looking frail and exhausted. I could hear the sound of voices floating in from the kitchen.

"Rachel, I'm so sorry. Can I give you a hug?"

"Oh, yes, thank you." She wrapped her arms around my neck and gave a squeeze. Then, stepping back and motioning for me to step into the foyer, she caught me off guard when she said, "You won't believe what he did!"

She went on with some animation to tell me that she woke around three a.m. and went to check on Robert. He woke to her touch and she asked him how he was doing. He said he felt fine and wanted to talk with her. She said they spoke about their early years, how proud they were of their daughter, and the love of a precious grandchild. She said he had always been so grateful for the blessings in his life, and this early morning talk was no different. Robert thanked her for being a great wife and mother and praised her for being a wonderful caregiver over recent years as his health had declined. Rachel said they talked for quite some time. Then Robert asked her to wake Carrie because he wanted to speak to her as well. Rachel had awakened their daughter and said, "Daddy wants to speak with you for a little bit. He and I just had the most wonderful conversation."

"Is everything okay, Mom?"

"He seems fine. He just wants to talk. Go ahead. I'll give you two time alone."

Rachel said her daughter went in and sat in the chair next to her dad's hospital bed. Robert told his daughter what an amazing young woman she had become, and how proud he was of her. He told her what a blessed gift his granddaughter had been in his life.

They shared some tears, hugs, and I love yous. They told each other how much they would miss being together. Carrie reminded her dad that he would always be in their hearts and never, ever be forgotten. She thanked him for being the most wonderful, loving, and supportive father and a great Papa to her little daughter. They sat quietly for a few moments holding hands, then Robert asked her to call her mom to join them.

Mother and daughter sat in silence as he rested, off and on, opening his eyes to look at them. Robert asked his daughter to get some water for him. After she left the room, he looked at his wife and asked if she would bring him a Tylenol for a mild headache.

In the kitchen, mother and daughter briefly spoke about what amazing conversations they had shared with him. They hugged and cried and said how much they were going to miss him—husband, father, and patriarch of the family. Returning to Robert with the water and Tylenol, they found him peaceful and motionless, his eyes closed. His wife noticed his chest was not going up and down; he wasn't breathing.

Rachel reached over and took hold of Carrie's hand and squeezed it. She said she wanted to prepare her daughter for what was happening. They walked hand in hand toward the bed. Rachel reached out and gently lifted Robert's hand into hers. Much to their astonishment, he opened his eyes. He looked at the two of them staring back at him and smiled. He whispered, "I love you all, so very much." Then he closed his eyes again, and they waited for another breath that never came.

The two women stayed with Robert and took in the unbelievable hours they had just spent with him. They were in awe of his peaceful passing—his ability to say I love you and then let go of life. What a powerful lesson in dying Robert had given to his family. I call this a lasting gift that will affect generations to come.

Robert had made his journey with orchestrated precision, thoughtful about how his death would affect his wife and daughter. He passed easily right before their eyes. Very few people are able to die the way Robert did, in such an unusually lucid way. Make no mistake in attempting to understand this phenomenon. Robert had worked hard to get his life in order so he could be at ease. His goal was to know he had done everything he could for his family before he left them. I imagine this peace is what allowed him to choose his time with such precision.

When I visited the home for my follow-up visit, Carrie shared an incredible story with me. She said on the day Robert died, she and her husband told their two-year-old daughter that her Papa had gone to be in the stars. On the next afternoon, the family gathered to celebrate Robert's life. The child was running about, playing and chatting to herself in the few words she had at her young age. She picked up Robert's picture from the coffee table and pressed it to her heart. Then she raised it above her head and, with a big smile, said, "Papa twinkle, twinkle."

The family looked at each other in amazement. How wonderful that this little girl could put a loss into such a beautiful and joyful perspective. Carrie said she knew how happy that small tribute would have made her father.

THE GIFT OF GIVING

*D*oes it take practice to die? Like many of the patients I have cared for, Jimmy made several practice attempts before he actually said his final goodbye and left his tired body behind. I would take his cue when he stopped eating and began to sleep all day. At that point, I would alert the family that he was entering his final phase—or so I thought.

The first time this practice attempt occurred, Jimmy had been in bed for a couple of days and had no interest in food or conversation. I told his wife, Susan, that this was usually a sign that the patient was beginning to make his way. This could go on for days; the exact timeline was hard to predict as it was a personal matter. I encouraged her to let the kids know, so they could come and say their goodbyes.

Little did I know that the house would fill to the brim with family and friends. That evening, there was a steady stream of people in and out of the bedroom—each one taking a turn sitting at Jimmy's bedside. Most were having teary conversations as they tried to say goodbye to the man they loved—husband, father, grandfather, uncle, brother, friend, and neighbor.

I expected to find Jimmy in bed the next day, well into his

dying process, but as I pulled into the driveway I saw him smack-dab in front of me, sitting in his lawn chair on the deck, smoking a cigarette. I let out a huge laugh and waved to him through the car window. He nodded and smiled back as a ring of smoke wafted above his head.

Boy, do I have a lot to learn, I thought. I shouldn't have been surprised by any of this. Jimmy was the patriarch of the family, and everyone relied on him for guidance and support. He was strong, and I had learned that he was the one who kept things on an even keel. Leaving his family would be difficult for him, and I had sensed by their reactions to my conversations with them that they were not ready to let him go.

The next time it happened, I found him sitting at the kitchen table having lunch. Once again, he had been in bed for a couple of days, not wanting to talk to anyone, not interested in food. He was busy doing the useful and necessary work he needed to do in order to prepare himself and his family for his death. The positive aspect of practicing to die is that it allows the family time to move closer to reality.

This man and his family taught me many great lessons. Their life was simple. They worked hard to pay their bills, and when one of them needed help another family member was always there for support. Caring for Jimmy when he became ill meant a paycheck would be lost if they wanted to care for him at home until he died. After a family discussion, his wife Susan chose to be the 24/7 caregiver, doing so with grace and acceptance of the struggles it would mean for them—emotionally and financially.

Jimmy's family was always incredibly kind and respectful to the hospice staff. They never put on airs and had no unrealistic expectations of what we could offer. Instead, they exhibited pure and honest gratitude for our care of Jimmy. The humbleness, kindness, and realness of this family made me a better person simply by being in their presence.

When Thanksgiving came, they all contributed a dish or two, so no one person carried the burden of all the cooking or paying for all the food to feed the large crowd. Susan said they were most thankful that year to have Jimmy at the table with them.

At each December visit, I wondered when they would put up their holiday tree. The week before Christmas, there was still no tree in the home. This broke my heart. Apparently, and with good reason, the hefty price of a freshly cut tree was not in their tight budget. On my drive home that evening I decided that, somehow, I was going to get them a Christmas tree. Although I was a single mom of three struggling with my own financial issues that Christmas, I knew it would make me so happy to give them the unexpected gift.

I remembered passing a roadside stand that was selling Christmas trees and wreaths. My plan was to see if Jimmy and Susan had gotten a tree by the time I made my next visit. If not, I would excuse myself in order to buy them one and return with the surprise. How fun! So, the next afternoon, I took fifty dollars out of my savings account and tucked it away in the small pocket of my wallet for safekeeping. Sure enough, a couple of days later there was still no sign of a Christmas tree.

I reviewed Jimmy's symptoms and medications, as usual, with him and Susan. After we finished our visit, I said, "There's something I need to do. Would you mind if I left and came back in a little while?"

Susan said, "Sure go ahead. Take your time; we're not going anywhere." They laughed together; no questions were asked.

I left quickly, excited about completing my secret mission, and drove to where I had seen the Christmas tree stand. I pulled in and my heart sank—they had packed up shop and all the trees were gone. Oh no, this can't be! I thought. Then I remembered that most roadside stands don't continue to sell trees so close to Christmas. I was deeply disappointed and knew I wouldn't find another Christmas tree stand anywhere nearby for the same reason. I looked around the empty lot, spotting a few *scraggly* trees left lying on the ground. I walked over to them and stood them up one at a time, but they would not do for this important gift.

"I hate to be picky," I said, speaking out loud to God, "but this is not what I had in mind for my gift."

A few scattered branches and small sections of cut-off trunks were lying around on the ground—a big mess left behind. I looked around, not ready to give up, and noticed the little trailer the staff had huddled in to stay warm. I prayed that someone would be there. I knocked several times but heard no response. Still hoping somebody was there, I knocked harder.

"Hello," I yelled, knocking even more forcefully.

No answer. I looked around again at the scattered mess and that's when I saw it. One Christmas tree wrapped in the plastic twine that makes it compact and easier for travel. I couldn't believe my eyes!

"It's for them!" I said. Then I looked upward. "Is this okay?"

The for-sale signs were gone along with the tables, and there were no homes or businesses nearby where I could inquire.

"I hope I'm doing the right thing."

I had to trust my instincts as I approached the lone tree and stood it up next to me. It was a tall tree, over six feet, and I wondered how the heck I was going to fit it into my little car.

"Okay, I sure hope you can help me with this next part, too," I said.

I walked over and opened the rear door on the driver's side of my little sedan and started to push the tree in trunk first. Much to my surprise, it went in easily. I was able to tuck the top of the tree inside with gentle bending. Then I shut the door and heard it latch.

"Thank you, God!"

A surge of incredible energy passed through me as I thought about what had just transpired because I had refused to give up. This reminded me that when you do things with an authentic, heartfelt purpose, they seem to work out in ways you could not have imagined. I was overjoyed and still perplexed about how the large tree had fit so easily into the back seat of my little car.

I knew there was more to my plan when I saw all the evergreen branches scattered on the ground. I thought they could make a lovely wreath or garland for the door, so I gathered the ones with nice shapes and put them into the trunk of my car. I was elated as I drove back to Jimmy and Susan's house.

I could hardly wait to deliver the tree to this wonderful and humble family, especially because it would be Jimmy's last Christmas with them. After I parked my car close to the house, I pulled that huge tree out of the back seat of my car with ease. I was still amazed that it was compact enough to fit. I carried it up to the deck and leaned it against the railing, then retrieved the branches from the trunk. I brought them up, laid them in a neat pile next to the tree, and knocked on the door.

"Come in!" several voices called out.

Their daughter Kara was there, so I said to the three of them, "I brought you a Christmas tree! I hope that's okay."

"You did? That's wonderful. Oh my God, thank you!" Kara just about bowled me over as she gave me a big hug.

I could feel her gratefulness and emotion. Checking my own emotions, I said, "I don't know what it will look like when you set it up—it's in plastic tree wrap. I sure hope it has a nice shape."

They thanked me so many times you would think I had given them a pot of gold. I was never so happy to do a good deed for a family as I was on that day. At my next visit, two days later, I saw the deck nicely decorated all the way around with tree branches. Their home looked absolutely beautiful! I knocked on the door, eager to see what the tree looked like out of its wrapper.

"Come in," two voices called out.

Inside the living room stood the most beautiful Christmas tree I had ever seen. It gave me goose bumps.

"Look at your tree; it's beautiful!" Susan said.

"It's your tree. It was just waiting for me to deliver it." We all laughed at the thought.

Jimmy and Susan reported that the children and grandchildren had enjoyed helping to decorate the tree. They told me they loved looking at the whole display with its beautiful lights. I could see that they had placed a few gifts underneath the tree, which indicated their anticipation of the upcoming celebration. I was holding back tears as I listened to their stories and witnessed how happy they both were—all from this simple gift that I had felt guided to bring to them.

A few weeks after the holiday, Jimmy began what we thought was another practice session—he fooled me again. This time it was the real thing and the family's hearts were better prepared. They were glad to have had the chance to celebrate another Thanksgiving and Christmas together. Mostly, they said they were pleased he could make his way with all of their love and goodbyes shared many times over. This gift he gave them was due in part to his need for practice sessions.

I never forgot this important lesson regarding the gift of practice sessions. It helps patients who have fears to take their time and gently step away when they are ready. At the same time, it helps loved ones prepare themselves, at least to some degree. As divine intervention would have it, I was on call the night Jimmy died. I was so grateful that I was the one to get the call and perform the pronouncement. I understood it was comforting for his wife to have my familiar voice at the other end of the phone.

"I'm so sorry, Susan. I am heading right out and will see you soon." I said.

As expected, the house was packed when I arrived. The large

family thanked me one by one that night. Susan and the children shared their gratitude for the hospice team. They appreciated all the care that the team and I had given Jimmy over the eleven months that we had visited. In turn, I told them they would never know the many lasting gifts they had given me. I thanked them for allowing me into their home and their lives during such a private time.

The next time I took my car in for an oil change, a funny thing happened. The clerk at the checkout desk retrieved my keys from the serviceman, and I could see the two of them talking and laughing as he passed them to her. When she returned to her desk she chuckled and said, "I have to ask you something. Did you put a Christmas tree in the back seat of your car?"

I smiled, realizing my car had been vacuumed as a courtesy, and said, "I did, and that tree was over six feet tall!

"No way! You fit a six-foot-tall Christmas tree in the back seat of that little car?"

"Would you like to hear the story?" I asked, knowing I had already piqued her curiosity.

She laughed again. "Sure."

Without using any names or locations, I shared the story. The young woman listened intently. I could see she was tearing up as I went on, and I started to get a little choked up myself. When I finished, she wiped a tear from her cheek.

"I love that story! Can I share it with others?" she asked.

"Sure you can. It's a true story of Christmas."

Each time I returned for an oil change, she always remembered me.

"You're the Christmas tree lady," she would say, smiling at me.

"Yes, I am. Thanks for remembering me," I would respond with a sense of honor and joyful memories of Jimmy, his family, and the miraculous Christmas tree.

8

FOREVER ON THE FARM

*A*lex was a well-educated ninety-year-old gentleman who lived on a beautiful mountain property in the country. The circa late-1800s two-story farmhouse boasted a wraparound porch with a view of a large meadow. The stone walkway with moss-filled spaces led me to the porch. A tall, thin man in a light-blue Oxford shirt peeked through the window of the door from behind his thin-rimmed oval spectacles.

"You must be Ellie?"

"Yes. Mr. Chopin?"

"Please, Alex is fine. Do come in."

He held the door for me as I entered his home and stepped into the dining room. I admired the stately long dining table with a disassembled Sunday edition of the *New York Times* scattered about at one end. I noted the camelback sofa with deep-gold upholstery—slightly threadbare on the arms and cushion fronts—and wooden claw feet that appeared to have walked a few miles. The sofa sat comfortably under the dining room windows, which overlooked the expansive meadow. Although the room was quite large, it felt cozy to me.

"Where would you like to sit?" Alex asked, glancing at the table and then the sofa.

"This admission process will take a few hours." I tossed the question back to him. "Where will you be most comfortable, Alex?"

"I think the dining room table would be best. I spend hours in this chair each morning reading the paper; this spot will be fine," he said, indicating the chair at the head of the table. "Make yourself comfortable."

"Thank you. It will take a minute for me to get settled."

I set my nursing bag on the chair next to me, and placed my laptop on the table with the admission packet on top. I rummaged through the big center pocket of my bag to retrieve the zippered pouch that held my nursing apparatus—pulse oximeter, blood pressure cuff, and stethoscope.

"May I offer you a cup of tea or coffee?"

"I would love a cup of tea. Thank you, Alex."

"Regular or herbal?"

"Any herbal tea sounds wonderful; I love them all. Surprise me," I said.

Alex smiled and headed toward the kitchen. I sat down on the comfortable cushioned seat and had to tug hard to get the heavy armchair to move forward toward the table. While Alex was in the kitchen, I glanced around the room like a detective gathering clues. I surmised he was an avid reader and committed to reading much of the *Sunday Times* because it was Wednesday morning, and the editorial section was folded back and lying open next to his half-empty coffee mug.

I could see another room toward the back of the house with a large bookcase at the far end; every shelf appeared filled to the brim. A leather recliner and small table with a reading lamp atop it sat next to the bookcase, suggesting this was another comfortable place for Alex. The remainder of the room was not visible from my vantage point. I wondered if, at his age, he was accessing the second floor of the large farmhouse or sleeping in a first-floor bedroom for ease and safety. I had many questions to put to my new acquaintance.

"Here we are."

Alex returned with a faded-green wooden tray. He had no problem carrying its weight to the table. He placed it down steadily before seating himself; unlike me, he pulled his chair up to the table with minimal effort. Decent strength for his age, I thought, as I continued in my detective role.

"I hope you like Lemon Zinger; it's one of my favorites," he said, sharing a small detail of his preferences.

"I love Lemon Zinger," I responded, making a connection.

Alex had many great questions for me as we began the admission process. First, he wondered if he was appropriate for hospice because he was feeling so good. I told him that in order for his doctor to have ordered hospice services, he must have felt there was a possibility Alex could die from complications of his disease in the next six months—one of the primary criteria for all hospice admissions. No one knew exactly the course his illness would take, and if he continued to decline, even slightly, and lived beyond six months, he could continue to receive hospice services indefinitely.

Finally, I ended with this: "If you continue improving, with no evidence of decline, then you will graduate from hospice. It's a well-kept secret that patients can choose to go on and off hospice services an unlimited number of times."

"You're kidding." He looked confused.

"There are many facets to hospice services that people are unaware of, including people in the medical community. This is a great example."

Alex said he liked having an understanding of how this "business of hospice" worked. He told me how much he appreciated my thorough explanation and ability to listen and explore some of his questions. He went on to say that he and his family had thought long and hard about whether he should pursue treatments before deciding against them. The treatments would only offer him a short extension of life and had the possibility of severe adverse side effects. Alex was sure he wanted to maintain a good quality of life for as long as possible. As we formed his plan of care, we agreed we would discuss his concerns with his physician before making any significant changes.

I was impressed by his ability to think about and explore his medical options. He chose to take time to consider his options rather than keep moving swiftly forward in the medical stream. I had met so many patients who learned of their diagnosis and hit the panic button, accepting any treatment offered, generally with little discussion about how it would affect their quality of life.

Alex wanted to ensure the time he had left would be the best it could be. He wanted to continue managing the only current symptom he had, tiredness. Alex said that several years earlier he had watched his wife decline from her illness until she died in the hospital from complications. For himself, and if at all possible, he wished to have less medical intervention than she had received. I felt honored to be the only medical provider he would choose to see regularly, an important role I understood would have its challenges. There was a depth of commitment to ensure I was getting it right for Alex, and on his terms.

Each time I arrived for my hospice nursing visit, I would find him either in his den or at the dining room table reading the *New York Times,* classical music playing in the background. He would greet me kindly but generally with no exuberance. It took a while for him to warm up to me and often my visits felt more like business meetings as I reported my findings after completing my nursing assessments. Then we would discuss the normalcy of his vital signs or the change if one had occurred. As time went on, I was able to continue to respond to his questions with honest answers or by offering to find the answers from my colleagues or his doctors.

This approach helped him build increased trust in me. This trust, coming from such a thorough and deliberate thinker, meant a great deal to me. I had so much respect for Alex's ability to contemplate and work through changes as they arose, subtle as they tended to be.

Many months passed, and he continued his unhurried but steady decline. During our weekly hospice team meetings, we had to discuss each patient's case and ensure we were providing all the necessary care. We also had to be sure each patient was still appropriate for services. When the question arose as to whether Alex was meeting the guidelines, his slow progression toward death sometimes challenged the insurance requirements.

Thankfully and sometimes artfully, I was always able to show sufficient evidence of his decline. Even simple things like a decrease in appetite or mobility and needing more assistance from the licensed nursing assistant (LNA), showed evidence that, although minimally, he was declining.

The hospice team knew full well patients could change on a dime and be gone in a few weeks or sometimes a few days. So, we struggled on the rare occasion a patient no longer met guidelines and had to be discharged, or as we would say, graduated from hospice services. Believe it or not, most of these patients were upset to learn they would have to be discharged. They had come to rely on the in-home support and guidance offered. Most appreciated hospice payment for their medications and the medical equipment provided to them at no cost. I found such discharges a silly bureaucratic practice, often causing significant stress to patients and their caregivers, especially since we readmitted most patients within a few weeks.

As Alex's trust in me grew, I was greeted with big smiles

when I arrived and began to stay to talk for a bit after my nursing assessments were complete. This private man was inviting me to socialize, and I can't begin to describe how good it felt to turn this corner with him. Suffice it to say, it felt like a great privilege to me. Finally, I was getting to know him on a personal level. He was interesting, witty, and quite engaged in life around him.

One day, I asked Alex if he had lived a good life.

"I have lived a great life."

He began to share more with me about his nine decades, his work, and his family. On one occasion, he told me he had been offering volunteer support, in his field of expertise, into his early eighties. He said he was traveling over an hour on public transportation to get to the meetings each week. That is, until they realized how old he was and promptly thanked him for his services and let him go. He laughed at his ability to appear younger than his years and fool them for so long.

Alex moved about easily and looked twenty years younger than most his age. I was not surprised they might have been shocked once they discovered how old he actually was and how far he was traveling. I imagine, once these details came to their attention, they saw him in a different light; in their eyes, he was no longer an asset, but a liability. Why do we assume as people age their vast knowledge becomes less valuable?

His children all lived out of state, which was often the case with many of our hospice patients. My communication updates were generally over the phone and at his request. I had quite a few phone conversations with his daughter, Grace. I had met her on two occasions when she stayed with her dad for a week and we had established a nice connection. I had met his son, Max, who came to stay frequently on the weekends, but did not have many opportunities to speak with his other two children. The four siblings communicated with each other and were all supportive and respectful of their dad's wishes.

Alex stayed as independent and active as possible over the many months I visited him. Most days he could be found reading in his den, sitting in the leather recliner with the seat that had a permanent suggestion of his shape. There, he would spend hours next to the bookcase that represented his love of reading. He read the paper or listened to his favorite National Public Radio programs. He continued going to the town library when he could get a ride back and forth from a friend. He said he enjoyed keeping abreast of the different aspects of town politics via the paper, phone calls with friends, or on a rare occasion, by attending an early evening meeting.

Eventually his disease slowed him down and as he became weaker he required help. In order to support him and ensure his safety, his children were able to arrange for several local people to come in to cook meals and clean the house. A woman named Marge came to make sure he got safely in and out of bed each morning and evening. He was still insisting on sleeping in the upstairs bedroom, and this meant going up and down the narrow staircase twice a day. With Marge at his side, he safely made his way, using the wooden handrail. Alex maintained his independence, for the most part, during the majority of each day.

Once I sensed he was approaching his final months, I asked Alex what his wishes were for the end of his life. Ensuring I had understood correctly, I confirmed that he wanted to remain at home with private caregivers and eventually support from his children for the final weeks of life. Alex told me he never wanted to leave his home of more than sixty years and the land he so loved. He said he and the children had already arranged for him to be buried on the property. I had never experienced a home burial before and was curious about the process. In those days, the early part of this century, it was not a common practice. Today, as the movement grows in popularity, anyone can go to a town official or funeral director to explore this option and arrange in advance for what is now called a green or natural burial.

As the summer went on, I noticed Alex was quieter, less inquisitive during my visits, and no longer interested in reading the *Times*. The latter fact alone told me he was becoming tired of living. When patients lose interest in the things they always loved doing, it is a sure sign of the beginning of the letting-go process. Alex was showing me he was preparing for his final weeks of life.

Clarice, the woman who cooked for him each night, had an important event coming up and Alex asked if I could cook for him in her absence. Knowing he could have had a meal prepared and left for him, I was honored by the request and happily agreed. Alex and I made a plan: I would conduct my nursing visit in the early evening, and afterward, I would stay to cook a simple dinner for the two of us.

I had been invited to lunches with patients and their caregivers many times over the years. These families appreciated being able to share a meal with their hospice caregivers; it was generally a gesture of gratitude. It took a while for me to learn to be comfortable as I graciously accepted those kind offers, knowing what it meant to the family. Leadership frowned upon staff using their time in this way, seeing it as unproductive, and if found out, we were usually reprimanded. I called partaking in these meals part of my passive resistance for a great cause—the human connection!

Once I was asked to join a couple for hasenpfeffer. The sweet husband, smirking, asked if I had ever had it, to which I replied, I had not.

"Oh, you must try it. It's a favorite of ours, and I do make a wonderful hasenpfeffer, don't I, dear?" he said to his wife with a chuckle.

"Yours is the best I have ever tasted, dear," she replied, a playful smile on her face.

I was a bit uncertain about the meal because of their spirited tone and tried to discern the flavors as I tasted the stew. There were chunks of tender meat in a thick, mildly spicy sauce, and I noted a touch of garlic.

"How do you like my hasenpfeffer?" the husband asked after I had taken a few bites.

"It's delicious. Thank you. I love trying new things."

Only after the meal did they share that the delicious dish was rabbit stew. I laughed and told them about a time when I was sixteen, and a friend and I had enjoyed a meal called Portuguese chicken only to learn it had been rabbit. I'd been fooled twice! They roared with laughter.

Alex requested a fish dinner, then politely asked if I had any food preferences. I told him I was not a picky eater and would love anything he chose. He suggested steaming the fish and having a tossed salad and a vegetable as side dishes.

"Sounds fantastic to me, Alex," I said.

He made sure the groceries were purchased for our dinner a day in advance, and we reviewed the plan during my midweek visit. I viewed cooking for him as a volunteer effort outside of my workday, and I appreciated the opportunity to step out of my nurse's role. I could tell he was looking forward to it as well, and I was happily anticipating our social time over a nice meal.

I arrived for my nursing visit at five p.m. sharp on a beautiful summer evening. As was our usual practice, I checked his vital signs, and then we discussed his current energy and comfort levels. He denied discomfort and admitted to greater exhaustion and napping for extended periods in his recliner in recent days. I told him these were expected changes and nothing of great concern. I suggested he appeared to be continuing his slow but steady decline. He agreed, saying he was so pleased to be enjoying his summer days in the home and on the farmland he treasured. He told me he was surprised he had lived so long—nine months since his admission. When we finished discussing his care, I told him I was going to begin preparing our dinner.

"I think I'll relax in my recliner and rest my eyes while you cook, if you don't mind," he said as he rose from the dining room table.

"That's a great plan," I agreed. "Get in a little catnap."

Alex surfed the furniture with his hands on the way to his den. I observed him as he stepped with more thought of foot placement and at a sluggish pace. Once I could see he was safely settled in his recliner, I headed into the kitchen.

I could feel a gentle breeze flowing from the front porch to the kitchen, pushing away the heat left in the house from the humid summer day. The cicadas were in concert outside the screened kitchen door. I enjoyed myself while preparing the meal in the old-time setting, peeking in to see if Alex was still fast asleep in the chair as I went along. After I had prepared the fish and washed and cut the broccoli, I decided not to start cooking the food right away; he looked so comfortable, resting his eyes, and I didn't want to disturb him.

As usual, I had a fair amount of unfinished nursing documentation to complete on my laptop, so I made myself comfortable at the kitchen table and picked away at the computer, closing out all my patient visits for the day. At about six p.m., I had finished and placed my laptop back in my nursing bag on the dining room chair. I tiptoed into the den and gently rubbed Alex's shoulder to wake him. "It's six o'clock, Alex. Will you be ready to eat in about twenty minutes?"

"Certainly," he muttered as he removed his glasses and attempted to rub his eyes into a state of alertness.

"Okay, I'll start cooking."

In the kitchen, I set to work on the built-in cutting board laced with hash marks, mincing a large clove of garlic and slicing a lemon, their scents mingling in the humid summer air. I turned the knob of the white porcelain stove to light the first burner; as soon as I heard the first pop the rotten egg smell drifted upward.

Alex appeared at the doorway, looking more alert now as he sat down at the kitchen table. As our meal simmered on the stove, Alex told me where to find dishes and glasses for the place settings. He motioned me toward the family-size salad bowl sitting on the counter, with its small cracks and uneven brown color.

He said he wanted to help prepare the salad, so I retrieved a small cutting board and a knife, bringing them to the table so he could chop the vegetables. I watched as he neatly and precisely cut the carrots in slivers and cucumbers in thin slices. Once finished, and with some effort lifting the board to the rim of the bowl, he pushed the vegetables off the cutting board using the back of the knife. He tossed the vegetables with the lettuces using salad tongs, then pushed the bowl aside. I thought the small salad for two looked lost at the bottom of the oversized bowl but did not say anything, as I understood tradition rightfully outranked practicality.

Alex commented on how nice it was to have a dinner guest and asked if I would like to split a beer with him. Since I had already closed out my nursing visit on my laptop, I said, "I'm off duty, and I would love to share a beer with you."

"I haven't had one in ages, but keep them in the refrigerator for visitors," he said.

"I do the same," I admitted with a smile and a nod, and went to get the beer before checking the pans on the stove. "I think dinner is ready."

A true gentleman, he complimented my cooking saying the food was delicious, and said the cold beer tasted great.

"I'm so glad we can share this meal," I told him.

"It's nice to have a dinner guest. It's been too long."

"It's nice for me too. I eat alone when my kids are with their dad. I think it's much more enjoyable to eat with company. And I'm glad to have this time to spend with you without needing to rush off to another patient visit."

At that, he raised his beer glass, and I followed suit as we clinked them together in a toast. "To friends," he said.

"Yes, to friends." I was honored to be put in this category in his life, realizing he would never know how much the kindness meant—a lasting gift and privilege.

By seven p.m., we had cleared the table; he had carried all the dishes and placed them in the deep sink. I washed them, enjoying the warm water and the view from the window. With care and no rush in his effort, he dried them and put them away. Afterward, the country kitchen was back in order—to his liking.

He smiled and said, "Great teamwork, Ellie. Thanks again for cooking."

"Thanks for treating me to dinner and a beer. I haven't had a beer in years."

"Oh, are you a wine drinker? he asked. "We could just as easily have had wine."

"I'm not a big drinker of either," I said, "but the beer tasted so good on this warm summer night. I really enjoyed it."

He nodded, then moved with effort into the dining room, again surfing the furniture with his hands to stabilize him as he went. He said he planned to relax while he waited for his nighttime caregiver, Marge, to arrive. He noted the beautiful colors in the sky as he passed the large dining room windows overlooking the meadow.

"Look at that sky. Just gorgeous, isn't it?"

"Yes, the colors are fantastic tonight," I agreed.

The sun was slowly making its way toward the horizon, and the sight made me think about our dinner conversation and Alex's appreciation for the simple joys of life. I recalled watching him move cautiously about the kitchen afterward. Now, it seemed to me, my friend was mimicking the sky as he made his own way toward the horizon.

"You must see some gorgeous sunsets out here, Alex. I imagine the stars are bright, so far from any city lights," I said, focusing on the beauty of nature and the joy it brings to life.

"Yes, the sky seems to go on forever on a clear night. My wife and I used to enjoy sitting on the back porch overlooking the fields as the sun set. Sometimes the colors were magnificent, like a Monet painting."

I noted a pensive look on his face and wondered what emotion his memory evoked. He rarely spoke of his wife. Was he thinking about seeing her again? Did he miss her? He was much too private a man for me to inquire so I left him to his thoughts. When he came back to me with a smile, I said, "Oh, that sounds wonderful. I love sitting on my deck at dusk and watching the dragonflies buzz overhead before the stars appear. We have no streetlights in my town either, so the night sky is beautiful and bright."

"We are fortunate to live in such beautiful country settings."

"We sure are."

"Thank you again for cooking."

"Oh, I enjoyed cooking in your lovely kitchen. Thank you for asking me. I hope you aren't feeling too worn out from doing all the dishes."

"Oh, no. I'll be ready for bed once Marge arrives at eight. That's not unusual. Early to bed, early to rise on the farm, you know."

"Of course, and a good way to live. Can I get you anything before I go?"

"Just my hug." He smiled as he turned to share in our latest ritual which, much to my surprise, had begun a few weeks earlier,

"I would never forget your hug!" I wrapped my arms around his back and gave a gentle squeeze; he squeezed back in the same manner. "I suppose I'll be off then," I said as I looked him in the eyes, noting he looked exhausted.

"Drive safely," he said, holding my shoulders as a concerned parent might do before their teenager left home for a Friday night adventure.

"I will." I smiled, touched by his sweetness. "I'll be back on Friday morning."

"I'll look forward to seeing you then."

"Okay, I'll let myself out. Good night. Thanks again for a lovely evening, Alex."

"You're welcome, my dear."

I stood in the dining room next to the table, and once I saw he was safely settled in his leather chair, I hoisted my nursing bag over my shoulder and headed out the porch door. The rugged hinges gave a loud creak goodbye as the door closed behind me.

I drove home with my car window down, refreshed by the cooling air. When I arrived in the center of the town, I listened as I drove over the old wooden trestle bridge. I loved crossing over and hearing the music, a sort of singsong reply to my tires touching down. As I continued on my way, I watched in awe as the colors changed in the wispy clouds above the horizon. I thought about the beauty in the evening sky, Alex's great company, and the blessings of my work—each thought filled my heart with joy. I appreciated having deeply meaningful and satisfying work, unable to imagine another job could offer such rewards. Before too long, I was home and settled on my deck to watch the last few dragonflies whiz by before the stars popped out.

About a week later, Alex became too weak to go up and down

the steep staircase twice a day. He told me he was aware of what the change meant. He accepted the time had come to move the bedroom downstairs and admitted he was tired and ready to die. Alex said he had enjoyed a great life but found little pleasure in his days any longer. He suspected this was a good sign that the time had come for him to move along. I was impressed with his acceptance and wished more of my patients could come to such a place before they died. I asked if he had any concerns he wanted to discuss with me. Was he worried about anything? Were there more things he needed to get done before he died?

"I'm not afraid to die. All my affairs are in order and the kids know what to do," he said, quite matter-of-fact. I was relieved to hear this, yet selfishly sad to think our friendship was coming to an end. His trust and confidence in me were meaningful; Alex was not an easily impressed man. I thought again about how I appreciated the gift of knowing him.

I remembered, on the day of admission, Alex's children had requested I let them know when he was approaching his final days. I told them I would do my best to keep everyone abreast of his decline but said it wasn't always possible to know when the last weeks or days had arrived—at least not with great certainty. But Alex had made this easy for me. I didn't have to guess.

His daughter Grace arrived within days and planned to stay with him until he died. She was a thorough and confident caregiver, their relationship was comfortable, and this was reassuring for her dad. Over the many months I had known him, he had spoken of his children with great pride. I wondered if he talked to them in this same way, being from a generation that often did not share such thoughts or feelings out loud. I really couldn't ask them directly, but wondered and hoped they knew.

With his children around him and accepting of his impending death, Alex began talking less, sleeping more, and having no interest in food—all the usual end-of-life behaviors. I was grateful

I was working on those last days to support them as he made his way toward death. The house felt joyful with his classical music playing softly, his children gathered around reminiscing about life on the farm and attending to his needs with loving care. On the afternoon Alex died, I arrived to find the children teary and grateful for what they called his peaceful passing. I told them how he had often talked about them with love and pride.

Alex's wish to never leave the farm was going to come true. Grace and I gently bathed and then dressed him. We placed him in one of his typical classy yet casual outfits. He was still a handsome and dapper man at ninety-two.

The family had planned for Alex to be viewed at home over the next two days. No funeral home involvement would occur until the day they buried him. Many friends and family were in and out of the calm and joyful house, sharing stories and food as they celebrated him and his long life. On the third day, the funeral home director arrived in the morning with a pine box, simple in appearance. His sons helped to place Alex's body inside. Then, with the help of his grandsons, they carried him out, and Alex left his treasured home for the last time. The men carefully maneuvered the narrow steps of the side porch and the stone walkway as they walked him toward the hay wagon that was attached to the team of horses. The late morning dew was on the tall grass in the meadow, and the buzz of insects filled the air. A group of about twelve family members and a few close friends stood off to the side of the porch watching as the unique memorial unfolded. I stood among them, imagining this home had similarly bid farewell to many others in its two-hundred-year history.

His elder son drove the wagon through the field and down the lane. The group of mourners followed quietly behind on foot. Being a part of this procession was quite emotionally moving for me. I appreciated being extended an invitation to such a private ceremony and powerful ritual. As we walked, and the bright sun warmed my face, I could feel my friend's genuine kindness and love surrounding us all. I snapped a wildflower as we walked through the meadow.

Once down at the gravesite, some brief words and prayers were shared. The casket was lowered deep into the ground, and no matter how many times I've witnessed this, I still get chills. The reality of death undeniable, a human soon to be covered by the great Earth for all eternity, in a final resting place we call a grave. A body all worn out and spent from life, and a spirit set free once again.

The family asked that we drop a flower, a rock, or a handful of dirt into the grave opening and onto Alex's casket. I said a prayer of thanks for having known him and his trust in me—and the honor of being called his friend.

"I will never forget you, Alex," I said out loud as I stepped forward to drop the wildflower, watching it twirl as it fell down, down, and rested on the pine box. It seemed fitting Alex would now rest beneath the Earth, the very same Earth he called home for more than sixty years—his beloved farmland, the place that had afforded him a long and satisfying life. Of all the amazing wakes and funerals I have attended, this was by far the most moving and touching authentic celebration of someone's life I have ever witnessed. It was thoughtful, profound, and unique, like the man I had come to know.

9

SAIL ON

How can a person look perfectly healthy and be unaware he is dying? Even after decades of caring for dying people, and having met several in such circumstances, I still ponder this question.

I thoroughly reviewed the hospital discharge paperwork prior to his urgent admission, and I fully expected a severely debilitated patient, in bed, looking close to death. David was in his mid-fifties, a fit and active man who enjoyed sailing, gardening, and hiking. He had recently returned from a month-long hiking excursion along part of the Appalachian Trail. He had enjoyed not only the beauty and solitude as they crossed the mountains, but also the physical workout required for long days of hiking.

Days after his return, he collapsed at home while mowing the lawn and was rushed to the hospital. He underwent several days of tests, and diagnostics revealed he had advanced cancer. Since he had been otherwise healthy all of his life, he and his wife Debra were shocked to learn the doctor believed David would be dead in a matter of days.

The medical team told them there was nothing more they could do for David at the hospital. They had made a hospice referral and said a nurse could meet them later that day, at home, to admit him to services.

When I met them that afternoon, I found David and Debra were still in shock and having trouble wrapping their heads around the devastating prognosis—they said it was like a bad dream. David was not frail, lying on his deathbed the way I had pictured him. He appeared fit and healthy on the outside.

I asked David questions about whether he had experienced pain or downplayed symptoms in recent months. He admitted he had experienced pain and tiredness but thought it was from overdoing it in the yard and garden.

I had, to that point in my four-year hospice career, never encountered such a young, healthy-looking patient with such a short time to live. David shared a photo of him taken during his vacation the previous week, arms stretched wide with the beautiful mountains behind him. I was having trouble wrapping my own head around this conflict as I looked at these polar opposites—a man joyfully embracing life and a man forced to face impending death. How can this be possible?

It rocked me to the core to imagine returning from a beautiful vacation, falling ill, and waking in the hospital to the news that your life would be over in a few short days. It made me queasy as I listened, and it made me want to ensure I was taking nothing for granted in my own life.

In these moments, no matter how much death you've witnessed, you can't help but feel a fear of the unknown and respect for the fragility of life—your own life. These patients, their stories, and their courage to face these unwelcome paths touched me deeply.

My work as a hospice nurse helped me to see what mattered in my life, discovering what brought me joy and what depleted my joy. These realizations made me want to avoid people who engaged in gossip, bullying, money worship, and the like.

Surrounding myself with the people who were important to me, the simplicity of my home and lifestyle, and the natural beauty and peace of my country backyard were some of the pieces of my life I recognized as joyful. Patients like David taught me to stay focused on what really matters.

I worked quickly that afternoon to get the necessary medications and equipment ordered for David, knowing his time was short. After we completed his hospice admission, I told David and Debra I would call the next day to check in and offer support, then visit them in person on the following day.

Upon my return to their home, two days later, I met many of David's friends and family, all coming to say goodbye, all shocked that David was dying. Every person I met, without exception, told me David had been a great support, great teacher, best friend, or had changed their life in some positive way.

When I sat privately with him at his bedside on the fourth day after his admission, I said to him, "I've met many of your wonderful friends and family. They all tell me you have taught them or helped them in some way."

"Oh well, that's kind of them. I like helping people, always have," David responded humbly, shrugging his shoulders.

"It seems to me you have an amazing spiritual presence."

"I have a spiritual presence?" he asked.

"It seems to me you do. You apparently possess wisdom you've shared with many people. I'm intrigued you were unaware," I told him.

"I never thought about having a spiritual presence. Tell me more; I'm curious."

"It's just my word for it. You might call it love, God, knowingness, or compassion. All I can say is I think you are about to meet your great spirit." I smiled at the look on his face.

David laughed. "Interesting. I'll let you know if I do."

We went on with our conversation regarding his comfort,

sleep, and the possibility of dreams or visions of deceased loved ones. I explained these were quite common at the end of life. I warned him that he might experience a decreased interest in socializing, and that food might lose its appeal. I reiterated that all of these possibilities were normal and expected as he made his way through his final days.

Although he didn't know it, David had a lot of work to do before he died and little time to do it. I had to offer a lot of information more swiftly than I usually would, and I wondered how a man who was unaware of his innate wisdom would be able to accomplish so much deeply meaningful work in such a brief period—work that often takes others weeks or months.

When I visited the next afternoon, Debra reported that David had refused solid food, only wanted liquids, and had slept a good part of the day. I reviewed the normalcy of all of this with her as reassurance he was doing what he needed to in order to prepare to die. I said he was busy doing his *life review* as he rested, and it was a useful and necessary way to spend his time.

The more I explained to her about the concept of life review, the more she recognized his efforts. She said he had been talking a lot about his life and what was important to him at different stages. She had noticed quite often in recent days how David was reaching his arms out and talking in his sleep. I was relieved to learn he was making progress in his journey and preparation to step out of this world.

Daily visitors had slowed dramatically as we neared the end of the first week. David was not able to expend the energy and time required for the emotional visits; their country home was getting quieter. David and Debra had been afforded more private time for talking. Debra said she was learning essential details about the new responsibilities she would have once David was gone. She was grateful they had discussed them before he could no longer provide her with the information.

They were a good team and had a calm and natural way together. As they discussed the household and financial details in depth, Debra said she felt overwhelmed at times. David helped her by saying it was necessary for his preparation to find his peace and leave the life he so loved. The more she understood and could take from his plate, the less David worried about her and the calmer he said he felt.

I was amazed he was not talking about the unfairness of it all. His short bout of anger came early and passed quickly; his concerns were for his family, not for himself—another example of his great wisdom.

On the seventh day, as I visited with Debra, she gave me the twenty-four-hour update and said David had experienced a restless night. I told her there were medications in the hospice comfort kit to help David relax if it became necessary. After I showed them to her, she thanked me, then said she wanted to get a few things done while he slept.

"Help yourself to some tea from the teapot on the kitchen counter."

"That sounds good; I will. Thank you."

I poured myself a mug of peppermint tea and headed to the bedroom, where I found David fast asleep. I sat quietly in the chair by the bedside as he slept. I began my nursing assessment by counting his respirations, noting his skin color and nail bed tone, and gently feeling his radial pulse at the wrist. Nothing unusual to note—he did not wake to my touch.

Once I had gathered all the medical assessment data I could without waking him, I sat in the silence and thought about the previous week and the flurry of visitors who came from near and far to say goodbye. David had somehow accepted his bitter pill with incredible strength and courage, rarely showing any trepidation or anger. I was in awe of him and still felt waves of fear when I thought about another human being learning, out of the blue, their life was limited to days. I hoped I was doing everything possible to make his short journey more bearable. I was deep in thought when his voice brought me back.

"Hi, Ellie. I didn't hear you come in. When did you get here?" he asked, rubbing the sleep from his eyes.

"I arrived about half an hour ago and talked with Debra for a bit before I came in. She said you were up a lot last night, and since you were sleeping so peacefully, I didn't want to disturb you."

"I don't remember being up in the night," he said, his gaze drifting toward the window as if the memory waited out there for him. I sat still, hoping he would recall any feelings or worries that may have been keeping him awake. After several minutes he turned to look at me and with a soft smile said, "I think I met my spirit last night."

"Really! How did that feel?" I asked, as I had envisioned it to be the size of a whale.

"It's funny, I thought it was strange when you said it, but I understand now," he said.

"Can I ask you if it was unsettling or comforting to you?"

"I would say it was definitely a comfort, and I can't fully describe it, except to call it familiar." He patted his chest twice as if to suggest it resided there.

"If you are interested, I can share with you what many other patients have taught me."

"Please, I'd love to hear it."

"Many say that, to some degree, this is what offers them peace and guidance. Everybody describes it uniquely, and I think I'm learning it is what ushers us into life. If we choose to be aware of it during our lifetime, it is there for us. Regardless, it emerges at the end of life to usher us out." I watched David as he digested the message from other dying patients.

"That explanation makes sense to me now. I find it interesting

I wasn't aware of it previously. You're full of new ideas for me to think about, Ellie." David smiled and reached for my hand. "Thank you," he said. I was surprised by his acceptance of his newfound existence within and humbled by his gratitude.

"I should be thanking you. You've made me do some reflecting of my own, and I can promise I will never forget you or your story, David. I'm sorry you've had so little time." The last sentence was snagged by my emotions, and I had to clear my throat.

"How long do you think I have?"

Ah, the million-dollar question, I thought, wondering if my emotions would trip me up again.

"I can't say exactly. You actually would know better than I."

"What?"

"I can explain it with symbolic examples, one that came to me and one I learned in my hospice training. Will you indulge me?"

"Of course. I'm curious."

I took in a deep breath, as my mentor and teacher had taught me to do before embarking on meaningful conversations. I gently let it out, releasing some of my emotions.

"In my symbolic example, you are walking on a path of stepping-stones as you approach the end of life. Each stone has a purpose. As you stand on each stone, you review the purpose and the memory it represents. You don't move forward to the next stone until you are ready for the next lesson or memory. Sometimes people step forward and then backward briefly. Eventually, and at their own pace, they walk forward on the path of stepping-stones."

"What is at the end of the path?" David seemed eager for an answer.

"The symbolism I learned in my training."

"Okay, let's hear it."

"There is a ship waiting at the shore, and it waits there only for you. Your family and friends remain onshore. You begin to leave the shore, looking back frequently to see those you are leaving behind. You continue forward on your journey toward the horizon. Sometimes you are pulled back toward the shore. This happens when the caregiver's words or emotions affect you. Also, physical interactions, such as repositioning or medication administration, briefly disrupt your course. Soon enough, you continue on your journey again. At your own pace, you will reach the horizon, and when you are ready and able, you will turn to say goodbye and then make the crest." I let out a quiet sigh, grateful to have made it through without getting choked up again.

"I like that." David smiled. "Honestly, I am more concerned about everyone else than I am about myself. Is that unusual?"

"No, it's quite common. Often there is one person patients are most concerned about, and this worry can hold them back. Sometimes patients need to hear from that person that it is okay to leave them. Patients tell me once their family seems ready to let them go, they, in turn, feel ready to die."

"I don't think I'm worried about one person. Debra is strong, and we have a great supportive family. When I first learned I was dying, I wished I had more time to get things in order. It was a weird feeling, as if a thief were stealing my life —a thief of time. I was angry in the hospital at the doctors and nurses who shared the sad news with us. Somehow, I don't feel that way anymore; I let go of what I couldn't control. Just getting through each day has been exhausting ... I've never slept so much in my life."

"You have been pretty busy, David, laying so much to rest in your heart and mind. It's exhausting work in and of itself. No one tells us dying is hard work. The fact that death is such a taboo subject is, in my opinion, a terrible injustice. You have done remarkable work and in a very short period of time."

"What happens next? How long will I go on? I know you said I know better than you, but I don't feel like I have any answers."

I shifted myself more squarely on the chair to face him, and this time I reached for his hand. He held on gently, looking directly at me, and nodded as if to encourage me to go on.

"The stepping-stone symbolism means you will go forward at a pace you set. I've learned that death does not steal you away at this phase; you are gaining comfort and acceptance and will pick your time to die. We have more control over death than we realize. So, please don't be afraid."

I paused to let the thoughts settle in. David squeezed my hand and nodded; I noticed his eyes watering a bit. "Thank you," he said.

"Would you like to hear more?" I wanted to be sure he was ready for more details of the changes he would experience in his final days.

"Yes. It's helpful to talk about what to expect. I feel less fearful when you explain it this way, and I like the symbolism."

"I'm glad this is helping you, David." I paused before embarking on the next portion of the conversation. "In the coming days, you will continue sleeping more, talking less, and only wanting sips of liquid, though you will continue to have an awareness of what's happening around you."

"Really?"

"Yes. Even when you feel too weak to converse, you will always hear your family around you. I'll do my best to keep you comfortable throughout. Most important is that when you are ready, you will decide who is at your bedside, or maybe you will choose to go quietly on your own."

"Hmm. What happens after I die?"

He was brave to ask such a question, and I mustered my courage in order to go on. I was still holding his hand, and I held on a little tighter in an attempt to give him strength and push back my emotions so my words would flow eloquently.

"I always tell families there is no need to rush in calling

hospice at the time of death." I found my discomfort rising. It was awkward to talk with a patient about what happens immediately after his death. But I knew I had to honor his wish to know the details.

"I'll ask your family to take all the time they need for privacy and to invite people into the home, if that's their wish, before calling for a hospice nurse to pronounce. Some may prefer to see you here one last time. When the hospice nurse arrives, he or she will offer to get you cleaned up and dressed in your usual everyday clothing. It appears to be comforting for the families who accept the suggestion. If you don't want us to provide this ritual, we will, of course, respect your wish."

"No, I would like to leave looking my best, all things considered." He shrugged his shoulders.

"Okay, David, I'm glad to know how you feel about that. When your family is ready, I'll call the funeral home and arrange for them to come. While we're waiting, I'll clean up in here and destroy the remaining medications. Then I'll make calls to arrange for the equipment to be picked up as soon as possible. Finally, I'll give your family time alone with you." I paused, grateful for having made it through the explanation without crying.

"That helps me. How the heck are you able to do this every day? Isn't it depressing?" he asked.

"I'm asked those questions quite a bit. I can't explain how gratifying it is to help people during these times. Yes, it is sad to meet a great person like you under such tragic circumstances, but, somehow, it also feels like a great privilege to be here. I appreciate being part of the circle of caregivers. It's rewarding when I help to ease some of the uncomfortable symptoms, fears, or concerns, especially when I can offer a sense of calm in the stormy moments."

"I can appreciate that," he said.

I let go of his hand and took in another deep breath before I made a confession.

"It also makes me see the fragility and preciousness of my own life. People like you teach me what matters in life is right now. I call this the no-bullshit phase of life. I prefer living this way as much as possible."

"The no-bullshit phase. That's a good description. There is no time for bullshit when you're dying, that's for sure."

"I can only imagine, David. I'm so sorry."

"I'm thankful you've been here with us. I'm surprised I'm teaching you anything, but I'm happy to be giving you something in return for all you've given to me." He smiled and nodded.

"It's my privilege to be here with you. It seems you've lived a good life and done an incredible job of having a positive effect on the world around you. If I had to guess, I would suspect you're still helping others. I imagine you're teaching your friends and family how to die with dignity."

"I don't know about that," he said, humble as always. "Will you be back tomorrow?"

"Yes, every day this week."

He looked over at the bedside table and pointed. "Would you grab the photo of me, please?"

"Sure," I said, as I reached for the photo of him with his arms stretched wide and the beautiful mountain ranges behind him.

"I would like you to have this to remember me by," David said as he handed me the photo. I choked back tears as I tried to think of how to accept the oxymoronic image of a man living and dying, a picture that truly captured a thousand words.

"Oh, thank you, David. It's a beautiful picture of your joy for life. I will keep it and always think of you and how you helped me remember what matters most in life."

I looked down at the photo, which seemed to be deceiving us, and shook my head in disbelief.

"I want to tell you, though, I will never forget you, even if I didn't have this picture to remind me. You are an amazing man with an incredibly huge spirit."

I stood up next to the hospital bed and bent down to hug him; he held on long.

"Thank you for everything," he said.

I stood up, nodded, and smiled as I looked at him. I think he knew I couldn't speak without letting emotion get the best of me and losing my composure. I held up the photo, then pressed it against my chest. I turned to find a folder in my briefcase to protect the gift, then gathered my computer and nursing equipment from the table and tucked them into my bag. Those few minutes gave me the time I needed to pull myself together.

"I should go so you can rest. I hope you have a deep and peaceful sleep tonight, David."

He nodded. "Me too."

"I'll see you tomorrow," I said, hoisting my bag over my shoulder.

He smiled, and I noticed his heavy eyes, as he waved his hand in my direction.

That was the last long conversation we had. What a gift it was and a day I still remember vividly. He stopped talking to his family the next day, answering them in a few words or with nods. David remained peaceful and comfortable for the most part as he worked his way out of this world. Two days later, ten short days after falling ill, David died just after dawn with his wife Debra at his side. Debra called family first and didn't call the hospice office until 8:30 a.m.

I was able to head right over and immediately, as I entered the home, felt a mixture of calm and sadness. A few family members and a good friend were present, and all said it felt surreal— David was truly gone from them forever. I spoke to his wife and offered her my condolences and a hug. I told her I thought she had shown amazing strength throughout the shocking and sad ordeal. She was holding up quite well and remarked she was glad David went easily.

After bathing him and dressing his lifeless body, I stared at the contradiction before me—a young, healthy-looking man, stone-cold dead. The truth sent a jolt of fear through my body. In silent prayer, I asked, Please help me to appreciate life and take nothing for granted.

I went quietly about my business cleaning the room, arranging for equipment removal, and destroying the unused medications. The family returned to spend some time with David before the funeral director arrived. As was my practice, I walked alongside him as the funeral director ushered him out of the house and gently placed him in the hearse. "Thank you, David. I wish you peace," I whispered.

I thought about the symbolism I had shared with David two days before. I hoped his journey with his newfound spirit carried him through a familiar passage—back to where he had begun.

10

HER WAY

Maggie had been referred to hospice by her oncologist. In recent months, several nurses had attempted to admit her; all had been unsuccessful. From my experience, when patients refuse hospice, it often has to do with the stigma surrounding hospice as service for those at death's door, while in fact, early referrals to hospice can lengthen patients' lives.

I had been told Maggie was difficult. In the medical world, that means patients are making their own choices; they are not doing what healthcare providers are suggesting. Being labeled difficult for making personal choices is unfair and disrespectful. I advocate for these patients and appreciate being able to help them make a care plan reflecting what they want for the remainder of their lives. It should not be a trip predesigned for them by the medical community. After all, this is their personal journey to the end of their lives.

Maggie and her sister lived in a cute cape in a seaport town. On my way to my first meeting with Maggie, I thought about this strong-willed woman and wondered how I would be greeted when

I knocked at the door. At this time, I had been a hospice nurse for seven years.

Maggie was a fairly tall, thin, short-haired woman, and that day she was dressed in jeans and a T-shirt. She was holding a little dog who bared his teeth and snarled at me. After she had calmed the chief of security, I introduced myself—I knew she could see my badge and understood the reason for my visit. She didn't offer me a smile; she just stepped to one side.

"Come on in."

There was a toughness about her, and I knew gaining her trust would not be easy. She sat in her favorite chair; I sat to her left, on the couch. The dog on her lap continued to bark at me. I sensed Maggie enjoyed the behavior because it wasn't making me feel welcome.

"What's her name?" I asked.

"Sassy."

I almost laughed. Seems about right, I thought.

"She's cute," I said.

"She can be if she likes you."

I smiled at the comment, knowing I would be lucky to get Maggie signed on and she was not going to make it easy on me. I set my briefcase down next to me and the admission packet on my lap, choosing optimism.

"I understand several other hospice nurses have come to meet with you to try to admit you to hospice services."

I let silence fall over the room as she stared me down, her eyes intense and beautiful at the same time. I could see she was enjoying the power of her past refusals.

"Yah, I think three of them. They all wanted to take away my Percocet. I'm not doing it," she said. "Why do you think you're going to be any different?"

"I would like to try," I said, with a smile. "Let's figure out what we can do to support you and your choices. I noticed in your medical record you chose to stop chemo treatments. Do you want to talk about that?" I wanted to learn more about her situation before she threw me out.

"Not really. They totally sucked, and I'd had enough. I'm doing pretty well now, other than the constant pain, and there's nothing we can do about it," she said, resigned to it after having endured the pain for years.

This sad scenario was something I frequently encountered during my years as a hospice nurse, and it was upsetting every time. Historically, doctors and nurses were not well versed in pain management—many physicians were guided by pharmaceutical reps in how to dose and manage their patients' pain. As we have learned in recent years, this didn't turn out to be an effective approach. Now, in the 2020s, the palliative care initiative has made great strides in increasing clinicians' knowledge base while providing greater resources to support them in their efforts.

Fortunately, I worked with a hospice medical director who was skilled in pain and symptom management. He went to great lengths to share his knowledge with any staff member or colleague who was interested in learning more and offered resources and mentorship to clinicians for decades. I was grateful for his teaching and used the knowledge I gained to keep patients comfortable.

I was surprised to learn many clinicians were unaware that different types of pain required a particular type of pain medication. For example, nerve and bone pain do not respond well to opioids, while a steroid like dexamethasone can do wonders. Knowing the appropriate options can save valuable time in finding the most effective treatment for a patient's pain.

I knew if Maggie would give us a chance, we could get her pain under control. "Well, I like to think there is always something more we can do. I'm not promising I can get rid of your pain completely, but I would love it if you would give me a chance to try to make you more comfortable, Maggie."

"I guess you want to take away my Percocet, right?" Her eyes flashed with fire.

"Why would I take away your Percocet? If you have pain, you need your Percocet. Maybe we can adjust the dose or frequency, instead."

"Are you telling me you're not going to try to take me off my Percocet?" She seemed annoyed, as if I were lying to her.

In an attempt to reassure her I said, "Yes, Maggie. I'm telling you I'm not going to try to take you off your Percocet, but we may have to consider what you could take for long-acting pain medication to give you better pain control. If you've been on Percocet for a long time, your body has become accustomed to it. Adding a different opioid can make a difference in better management of your pain. Different opioids speak to different pain receptors in your body. Using a product not in the oxycodone family as your long-acting medication will likely be beneficial for you."

"Really?" she said with sincere interest.

"Yes, really. Are there any other reasons you didn't want to be admitted to hospice?"

"Every other nurse I met wanted to tell me what I had to do, and how I had to take my meds, and what I could take and what I couldn't take," she said, exasperated. "And I don't want anybody coming in here and telling me how to live my life!"

"I don't blame you," I told her.

I loved her conviction and ability to maintain control of her world. We are going to get along great, I thought, not daring to suggest this to her in the heat of the moment.

"Let me tell you how I practice. I like to give control back to the patients. It upsets me when the medical community, my colleagues, try to tell patients what they should do, usually without asking them what they would like to do."

Maggie shot me a look of surprise.

"I think we should be telling people what all their options are and letting them decide what is best for them. If you pick an option I don't like, or one I believe may not be the best choice, I shouldn't discourage you as long as you've been well informed. Besides, people are also allowed to change their minds at any point if their choice no longer seems right."

She laughed. "No kidding," she said with a note of sarcasm. "I think I like you. I think we might actually get along."

As I looked at Maggie, I felt the barriers beginning to fall. Sassy was snuggled into her lap, off duty—I was no longer a threat. I respected Maggie's courage, feistiness, and ability not to give in until she got what she wanted.

"Yes, I think we could be a great team, Maggie, and I would love to help reduce your pain. It might take some time to figure out the best approach. Is that okay?" I asked, hoping she would consent.

"Having no pain would be amazing; I'm not sure you can do it, though. My oncologist couldn't. Don't get me wrong, I love him, but he has never been able to totally get rid of it."

I knew if I could make Maggie more comfortable, it would help her build trust in me and the hospice team.

"If you can trust us to try, we'll do our best. Our medical director is well versed in pain management and he has a very high success rate for helping patients reduce or eliminate pain altogether."

"I will give you and him a chance. How does it work, getting on hospice?"

We're in! I thought, elated and surprised.

"Okay then, what we'll do first is have you sign your hospice consent forms. This means you understand your oncologist is saying he believes there is a chance you could die in the next six months from your cancer or a complication related to it. Did he explain it in this way?" I asked, hoping for an affirmative response.

"Yes, he did. The reason he keeps calling you guys is because he can't control my pain. I love everyone in his office, and they're good to me. If I pick up the phone and call them, they get back to me immediately and are kind and helpful. I wish more people in the world were like them."

"So do I, Maggie." I smiled at her, thinking we had found another piece of common ground. "If you're agreeable and you want to sign these consents today, I'll do a full nursing assessment and review your medication list with you. Finally, I will order all of your current medications, and they should arrive in a day or two."

"What do you mean you'll order my medications? I don't need you to order my medications. I get them at the pharmacy in the grocery store around the corner."

"I understand; let me explain. Once you're admitted to hospice, according to your insurance—Medicare—hospice has to pay for your medicines. Anything that's related to the cancer is our responsibility."

"I won't have to pay for them?" She looked at me as if I were giving her a line.

"Not anymore, you won't."

"I better not run out!"

Sassy growled, lifting her sleepy eyes to look at me.

"I'll stay on top of it. We order about every two weeks. And you can call the office if you get low on your Percocet tabs and let us know you'll need them reordered sooner. Okay?"

Sassy snuggled back in to complete her nap.

"I guess so. We can try it."

She was clearly skeptical. Still, I was aware she was doing her best to trust me.

"We'll go over your medicines together today. Then, I'll order them from the hospice pharmacy," I said, making sure we were on the same page. "It's a good system; they ship them quickly, and they are delivered right to your door. The orders usually arrive the very next day."

"Really? So fast?" She seemed relieved.

"Yes. I'll need you to help me with the reordering of Percocet because you're using them as often as you need them, and this could change weekly." I wanted to reinforce that she would continue to have control of her Percocet.

We reviewed her consents together, and she signed them, reading them thoroughly beforehand. She already had a do-not-resuscitate (DNR) form hanging on the refrigerator, the location recommended by most hospice agencies. The DNR is generally a requirement for hospice admission; if patients wanted more life-sustaining treatment in the future, they would not be of the hospice philosophy and could not be admitted.

"Now let's talk about the long-acting medicines you have tried in the past. Have you ever tried MS Contin?"

"Nope, never tried that one."

"How about Oxycontin?"

"Nope, haven't tried that either."

"Have you ever been on a fentanyl patch?"

"No, but I think they gave me fentanyl in the hospital once, and I know they gave me morphine during and after surgery."

"All you use is Percocet, and you've never been on a long-acting pain medication?"

"Yes, Percocet and sometimes Tylenol or Advil."

Next, I needed to review short-acting medications, though not in an effort to use them since we had established that she wouldn't let go of her Percocet.

"How about Dilaudid? Have you tried it as a short-acting pain medication?" I was becoming more curious about what her doctors had been trying with such poor results.

"Yah, I think I did try it, but it didn't work as well. Listen, I've been on Percocet since the early 90s. There's no way I'm going to change after fifteen years."

I understood her anxiety, and imagined she felt she may have given up some control by signing on with hospice.

"Maggie, I hear you, and I can promise you I'm not going to take away your Percocet. But I need to know what you've used in the past to help guide me toward the best long-acting pain medication. I'll also need to know how much Percocet you're taking every day, to help me determine what you need for a correct dose. If you're receiving the appropriate dose of a long-acting medication, you'll use your Percocet when the pain breaks through. The long-acting should manage all of your pain, but we know there may be times when it doesn't, and that's when you use the Percocet."

"You sound like you know what you're talking about." She laughed. "I take two of my Percocet every morning when I get up, at bedtime, and at least once during the day. Why do I need the long-acting medication?"

"You don't have to change how you take the Percocet. Long-acting medications usually provide better pain management because they are designed to give relief over twelve hours. Once you're on a long-acting medication, you may find you don't need the Percocet at those same times every day. When you feel pain, then you can take the Percocet. I'm not going to tell you how to use your Percocet. I want to help you feel more comfortable. Nobody should be in pain every day, Maggie," I said, shaking my head and looking directly into her eyes.

Maggie's eyes watered, and we were silent for a minute. I knew she did not plan for me to see this emotion and could understand how compassion from a complete stranger was unexpected. In the silence, I think we both knew we were going to be great friends.

Teasing, and hoping to break some of the tension, I said, "Now that we're friends, tell me about your bowels. Did you know hospice nurses love to talk about their patient's bowel movements at every visit?" We both laughed. Sassy woke again and looked at me, no growling this time. I was making progress with the dog, too.

"Yeah, I take Colace every day, and it works for me."

"Okay, that's great. You probably know Percocet and other opioid drugs are known to cause constipation. The doctor who writes the opioid prescription should write orders for an appropriate bowel regimen," I said, sharing one of my hospice nursing mantras.

"I'll admit I've had some trouble in the past, but the Colace is really working well."

I was surprised and pleased she had shared some personal information with me; this was another good sign.

"We might have to increase it as we add another opioid. We can work together on this," I suggested.

"Okay," she agreed.

Hoping to give her as much control over her care as possible, I asked, "What time of day would you like to have visits?"

"You're not coming every day, right?"

I laughed. Not feeling the love just yet, I thought. "No. I won't overwhelm you."

"I don't want morning visits; I like to sleep in. Then I like to get up and drive down and get my Dunkin's coffee, and then I come home and chill out a bit. Visiting in the afternoon is better for me."

"Okay, you've got it. Sometimes, because hospice patients are unpredictable, my schedule changes. If a patient needs me, I do my best to get there quickly. In such situations, I call my other patients and rearrange the day."

Maggie nodded. "I understand. That's fine with me, and if I don't pick up, leave a message."

"I'm thinking, because we're starting off, and planning to do some medication changes—not your Percocet, of course—it would be best if I came a couple of times in the first week or two, while I monitor the changes. What do you think?"

She gave me an annoyed look and responded somewhat reluctantly, "Yeah, that's fine."

"Good. Afterward, we can go down to a visit once a week. Anytime you have questions, or you need anything, you should call the office. I can make additional visits when you need them," I said, trying to keep the control in her hands.

"Once a week is enough," she said.

When I arrived back at the office, they wanted to know how I had "tricked her" into signing the consents. This turned me off. I tried to keep emotion out of it as I explained I hadn't used tricks —listening to Maggie was all it took.

I was tempted but didn't bother to try to explain my philosophy of letting patients maintain control over their life by giving them information, choices, and options, and respectfully allowing them to choose the option that felt right for them.

When people become sick, like Maggie, they experience a devastating loss of control of the life they've known. Not being able to care for themselves or their home or continue to work in the same way they had been accustomed to, are all losses. It's scary and unsettling for most people.

I had learned early on how returning decision-making control to patients was one of the greatest gifts a hospice nurse could offer. Sometimes it broke my heart to learn of the choices patients made after being given their medical options. I would remind myself it was not my job to guide them in a direction aligned with my comfort level. It wasn't easy to come to this place of practice with my patients, but once I did, it made me a better nurse and advocate.

There were many times when I had to tell patients and families things the medical community had left out of the conversation. Knowing they were going to be angry at me—and basically, *shoot the messenger*—I still felt the information needed to be shared. Without knowing all of the pertinent details they could not make educated decisions.

I had met with countless oncology patients over the years who either didn't hear the oncologist say or weren't told that a referral to hospice meant having a prognosis of six months or less. Patients were also expected to have a do-not-resuscitate order (DNR). Having a DNR order meant if their heart stopped, no one would provide cardiopulmonary resuscitation (CPR) to attempt to restart it. If they stopped breathing, no one would attach them to a breathing machine. It meant when they died no one would try to bring them back to life or keep them alive on artificial life support.

When I reviewed hospice consents with patients and their families, I shared these details with them. Many patients had no idea this was the criteria they needed to meet in order to be accepted into hospice. Insurance companies require two doctors to agree that the patient has a six-month prognosis. The doctors must sign and attest that the primary diagnosis could lead to death on its own or, by some other complication in the next six months, and patients can no longer participate in curative treatments.

Those are huge pills to swallow in one sitting. It was disappointing to meet so many patients who had been in various medical settings where these conversations should have been taking place, possibly shared gently over time. Sometimes patients did have a limited understanding of the hospice philosophy and criteria, but rarely with full disclosure. In these instances, either the social worker or hospice nurse had to be the bearer of bad news. We also had to be the ones to explain the insurance criteria for admission to hospice.

Many patients are anxious about signing on for hospice services because to most it signifies the end, giving up, and a road to the unknown. Few are aware of the benefit of hospice services beyond the care offered by a team of professionals and the payment of medications and medical equipment. Patients live longer and with a better quality of life when hospice is involved.

Sometimes, patients were angry with us after learning of their prognosis. The term *shoot the messenger* applied time and time again. In those moments, when families were upset, I would often ask myself why I felt such a connection to the work. For me, it came back to the hospice team's ability to bring people to a place of trust and comfort, both emotionally and physically. It was knowing what we could do for them that gave me strength and resilience. I had learned how to stay the course, allowing them to vent their anger and fear—while trying not to let it penetrate me.

Over time, most patients and families came to have trust and respect for their hospice team members. They understood it was out of advocacy for them that we wanted to ensure they were fully informed. Knowledge is powerful.

Maggie and I worked together every step of the way. The medical director had started her on MS Contin 15 milligram every twelve hours after my first visit, and this worked very well for her. She continued taking her Percocet at the same times every day, as she always had.

Good pain management had not been difficult to attain. Best of all, she could feel the difference right away. She said she had more energy and felt happier than she had in a very long time. This is why I loved the work I was doing!

After many months, I was able to teach Maggie to use the Percocet only when her pain reached a three on the zero-to-ten scale. Going forward, I was better able to assess her pain by monitoring how much Percocet she was using. When she needed more Percocet, it indicated that it was time to increase her long-acting medication.

Hospice teams ask patients if they have a wish for something one more time, or maybe for the first time in life. It was rewarding when we could make wishes come true for patients—while they could still appreciate them. It might be something as simple as being reconnected with a loved one, or as elaborate as a final trip. One of my favorite social workers had an amazing ability to find grants, resources, and donations, making patients' dreams come true—no matter how grand. I used to say she was like having Santa Claus on the team.

At first, Maggie said she didn't have any wishes. But once we had built a good solid trust, she said she wanted to see her only child and grandchild again. They lived out west, and the trip would be costly. Additionally, her energy was not optimal for such a trip. I suggested having the social worker assist her, but Maggie declined, saying if she needed help, she would let me know.

Maggie also had family members who wanted to help her with her day-to-day responsibilities, but she consistently refused them too. Maggie had been a self-sufficient woman all her life and changing now was not realistic. Most people remain who they are until their last breath—only on a rare occasion have I observed people changing a longstanding belief or behavior at the end of their life.

From the first day we met, Maggie's blood oxygenation levels (O_2 sats) were in the mid-80s. This is considered low, and supplemental oxygen is generally recommended to help increase the levels into the 90s—normal range. I continued to suggest ordering oxygen, and Maggie continued to refuse, saying, "I don't want to drag a damn oxygen cord around with me all day!"

I respected her wishes. We were able to keep her breathing

comfortable and her pain under control as it increased by using medications. As the tumor on her shoulder grew and became more visible, she didn't let it stop her from going to get her morning coffee. She also continued to go to grocery and department stores for whatever she needed. On occasion, Maggie would mention how people stared at her.

"I'm not going to let it keep me in; I'm going to keep living. The hell with them! Let them stare!"

I think, deep down, it did bother her. But true to her tough nature, she would never admit to it. I had enormous respect for her strength and courage. I had known her for over a year and although nurses are taught to never make personal connections with our patients, I had grown to love Maggie like a friend.

Maggie didn't have a large social circle, but she did talk often about her best friend, Jack. The first time she told me about him, she was very emotional—she said they were soulmates. She told me that after he died, she had Jack's ashes buried out west, but kept a small amount to put into a necklace. She held the small glass cylinder up to show me, saying she wore it around her neck, keeping Jack close to her heart. I thought the sentiment was beautiful.

I was surprised to learn Jack was her beloved horse of many years. She often talked about the care she had given Jack, and the joy he, in turn, had given her. Riding him, she said, was a deep feeling of freedom like nothing else in her life.

I wanted Maggie to meet and connect with another nurse in order to make the visits easier when I was away on vacation. I told her I thought she would like several and grow to trust them, but she was reluctant. Maggie eventually felt a level of comfort with a licensed practical nurse (LPN) named Sara. She began to accept Sara's visits when I was away or when I had a last-minute schedule change due to a patient crisis. Sara was wonderful and acted as a backup for many of the registered nurses (RNs). Unfortunately, this meant she was in high demand and was not always available to visit Maggie during my week-long vacations.

Before leaving for a welcome diversion each spring and fall, I would ask Maggie to consider accepting a visit from the covering nurse in my absence, if Sara was not available. While I was gone, a colleague would call her to check in, reorder her meds, and try to set a visit. Being true to her stubborn nature, combined with a mistrust of the nurses who wanted to take away her Percocet, if it wasn't Sara, she would usually refuse. As hard as I tried not to think about work while I was away, I must admit I worried about her.

As a hospice nurse, I recognized that in order to avoid burnout, you have to get away. You have to take regular breaks to maintain the level of giving and caring that's required for the job. I made a practice of leaving the country once or twice a year for my own revitalization—somewhere tropical where I had limited-to-no cell phone service. This allowed me to relax without keeping me tethered to the fast-paced world—a necessary disconnect.

I understood the reasons for the choices Maggie was making, yet I was still concerned about her getting the best care in light of them, especially as her disease progressed. It is a beneficial practice for patients to get to know other members of the hospice team —that's why we are called a team. The team members hear about all the patients in our interdisciplinary team meetings each week. They know quite a bit about what is going on with each one, though the patient may not be aware of this fact.

During one of my vacations, a per diem nurse visited for a pain crisis. The first thing she attempted to do was change Maggie's medications by replacing her Percocet. One of my colleagues reported to me, "Maggie threw her out!"

I received a voice message from the per diem nurse stating she felt the Percocet was not right for Maggie. She suggested I change her to another short-acting medication. I agreed another opioid may have been better for Maggie, but we stayed with the Percocet for an important reason. Maggie had one stipulation when she signed on with hospice: "Don't take away my Percocet." I promised her I would honor her wish—never defying her trust.

I was frustrated. Even with my forewarning not to rock the boat with Maggie so as not to lose her trust in us, this nurse did so anyway. After I had learned of the interaction between them, I felt as if I had let Maggie down because I was not there to advocate for her.

Maggie told me the nurse was pushy and didn't listen to her. She was angry and I didn't blame her. I was grateful that Maggie and I were able to continue to have good communication and respect for one another after that incident. This relationship was longer than most because Maggie lived for almost two years as a hospice patient.

Her wish to see her only child and grandchild was partially granted a few months before she died, when her son came to visit her for a week. She had grown too debilitated to move around the house without effort, never mind take a long trip. I could see her body frame emerging, hear her efforts to breathe when she walked, and often caught her nodding off during our visits. Sadly, she was not able to see her grandchild again and this was heartbreaking for her.

During Maggie's final month, she didn't go shopping as much, yet never stopped going out for her morning coffee. She slept more, ate less, and was getting a bit confused. I wasn't sure if she was taking her meds appropriately, but, true to form, she refused to let me set up a medication planner for her.

Her family monitored her safety and supported her wish to be independent right down to the last. I suggested licensed nursing assistants to help her bathe when I knew she could not manage alone, but she refused. I've known many patients who stopped showering months before they died. Having a simple sponge bath was all they could handle, and they said it was enough for them. For the most part, these people remained clean and were able to maintain good skin integrity.

If patients develop skin breakdown and open areas, called bedsores, care becomes complicated. Not receiving proper care can lead to mild infection, pain, and sometimes sepsis—a severe blood infection that can be fatal. It's pretty amazing how patients who are physically compromised, like Maggie, are able to manage their personal care and daily routines on their own for so long.

I was a bit more concerned before leaving on my vacation this time around because Maggie was feeble, and I knew she would refuse nursing visits while I was away. I had been visiting her twice a week; on occasion, three times for symptom management. Since she was getting progressively worse, I strongly advised her to accept another nurse in my absence, but to no avail. I also had another concern. I did not know how to tell Maggie I had given my notice and would be leaving the agency in three weeks. I had accepted a position with another hospice agency in the area—a tough but necessary decision for me.

Maggie, in her private and independent way, never allowed social workers, spiritual care providers, or licensed nursing assistants to make a strong connection with her. I worried about how things would go for her if I had to start my new position before she died and was sick to my stomach just thinking about telling her. It was as if I was betraying her and my other patients by taking the new job. Despite these feelings, I knew the change was a healthy choice for my career, and I had to trust my instincts and hope, somehow, things would work out.

I could not imagine how Maggie would build trust with another nurse at the end of her life. It had taken us time to form a trusting relationship. Finally, after much deliberation, I decided to wait until my final week with the agency to share the news of my new job with my patients and their families. Maggie was in my care longer than any other patient, and I dreaded telling her I would be leaving the agency.

I returned from vacation on Saturday and was on call the next day—Maggie and her family knew this. The phone rang first thing on Sunday morning. Sure enough, it was the overnight on-call service reporting Maggie's sister Barb had requested a call-back from me. My heart sank. I wondered what had transpired while I was away. As hard as I tried to relax during my vacation and not think about work, I did worry about Maggie and a few other patients during my long contemplative beach walks.

I quickly returned the call to Barb, who told me Maggie had been in bed most of the week, and had not gotten up since Friday, which was unusual for her. Barb said what scared her the most was Maggie's acceptance of a bed bath on Saturday morning. This was the first time since her illness Maggie had ever let anyone help her with anything pertaining to the care of her body. Without saying a word, we both knew what it meant.

I told her I could make a visit right away, and Barb whole-heartedly accepted. When I arrived, Barb was waiting at the door to let me in. I was surprised when Sassy didn't greet me.

"Is Sassy with Maggie?"

"No, Maggie gave her to my daughter on Friday."

"Oh, I'm glad Maggie knows Sassy's in a good home. I imagine it's a relief for her."

"Yes, it was a tough goodbye, but necessary. Sassy was getting anxious. You won't believe how much Maggie has changed since you visited last week. But true to form, she drove down to get her coffee on Friday," Barb said with a laugh.

"I love her fortitude. Can I go check on her and then report back to you?" I was looking forward to seeing my friend but concerned about the condition she'd be in.

"Please do."

I found Maggie curled up on her side, in her bed, facing the window. I had never been in her bedroom, even though I had visited for almost two years. Generally, when I visited, she was in her recliner in the living room with Sassy snuggled on her lap. Those days were over.

I knelt down next to the bed and gently brushed her hair back from her sweaty forehead. I rested my hand on her cheek. She opened her eyes slightly, gave me a tiny grin, and said, "You're back."

I nodded and smiled at her; it was hard to speak. She sensed it and opened her eyes wider, looking directly at me.

"Am I dying?"

I nodded again. "I believe you are, Maggie. Are you ready?"

"Yes, I'm tired."

I took her hand. She held on, now with her eyes partially closed again.

"Are you in pain, Maggie?" I asked.

She nodded.

"It's time to get you on a fentanyl patch because you're not going to be able to swallow your pills anymore. Okay?"

She nodded again and whispered, "Thank you,"

"You're welcome," I said, holding back tears. She could hear it in my voice and kindly squeezed my hand, trying to give me some of her immense strength.

"You are one of the bravest, toughest, strongest, and most stubborn women I've ever met, Maggie," I said, with a tearful laugh. "It has been such a privilege to be your nurse." I paused to take in one of those deep breaths my great teacher had taught me to use in emotional situations like these. "Thank you for allowing me to help you to live out your life the way you wanted to. I'm here for you, and I will be coming every day now."

She nodded and squeezed my hand again.

"I'll be right back. I want to make a call to the doctor and get the fentanyl patch ordered." Before I stood up, I rubbed my hand across her cheek and held it there for a brief moment. Then I rested my hand on the crown of her head, silently transferring loving energy and calm for her upcoming journey. She looked peaceful in the *end-of-life way* patients do when they have accepted their death is awaiting them.

I tiptoed out and paged the medical director, who responded quickly. He was wonderfully supportive, knowing how long I had been caring for Maggie and our strong bond.

"Are you doing okay?" he inquired.

"I'm struggling a bit to hold my emotions at bay until I get back in my car. I'm using conscious breathing like Wil taught me, and it's helping for sure. Thanks for asking. I really appreciate it."

"You're welcome. What do you need?"

We discussed Maggie's current twenty-four-hour opioid dosing and calculated her equivalent fentanyl starting dose. He immediately faxed the order to the local pharmacy, which we used in urgent situations—not wanting to wait a day for home delivery. After five minutes, I called to see how quickly the pharmacist could have it ready. He knew Maggie well from many years of filling her prescriptions and asked if she was no longer able to swallow. I knew he was asking me if she was dying.

"She's transitioning," I told him.

"I can have the order ready in fifteen minutes."

"That's great. Thank you so much and thank you for taking such good care of her. Maggie often spoke of your kindness."

There was a brief silence on the other end. I understood his compassion and was grateful I could tell him he was appreciated. Once I hung up, Barb headed out to pick up the medication.

While she was out of the house, I went back in to sit at Maggie's bedside. I brought her up to speed, saying I would be placing the patch within the next thirty minutes. I took her hand and whispered to her, "Maggie, are you afraid?"

She answered softly. "Yes."

My heart sank, but I knew I had to find my strength and keep my composure. I sat up straight and filled my lungs, letting the tension go. I needed to dig deep into my courage to get through this conversation. I was thankful when my intuition took over, and the right words followed.

"Maggie, this journey is no different than anything you've done in your life. You have the knowledge, strength, and courage necessary to carry you through. I understand the unknown can be scary but trust your spirit to know the way; like the baby who knew how to be born, you know how to die. I have no doubt you're going to do this beautifully." I relaxed, unsure of where the words had come from.

"I'm going to keep you comfortable. Please let go of anything that's holding you back."

Maggie nodded. I rubbed her shoulder with my other hand, knowing the toughest part was over.

"If you have dreams or visions, ask the questions weighing on you and causing your fear. The people you are seeing will guide you. I can't help you with this part of your journey, Maggie. This is the spiritual work only you can do. Once you feel a deep peacefulness, settle into it, leave your tired body in the bed and let your beautiful spirit go."

Her eyes were closed—she didn't see my tears had made their way out and trickled down my cheeks; I caught them with my sleeve. The explanation was not creating any visible fear, and I was relieved for her. A woman who usually had some response was listening now. Her trust in my words was a huge privilege, one that I didn't take lightly.

"There's no rush, and doctors and nurses don't know when someone's going to take their last breath. You know better than anyone. You'll feel it, Maggie. You'll know."

I rubbed her arm in encouragement and comfort. She nodded, confirming she had heard everything.

"You'll continue to hear us, Maggie. Even when you're too tired to respond, you'll hear your family, you'll hear me. We'll be here for you."

"Good," she whispered.

"I know you're independent and don't need someone to hold your hand every minute, or to dote on you. Barb and I will work together to keep you comfortable. Does that sound okay?"

She squeezed my hand again and opened her eyes. "Yes."

Her glassy end-of-life eyes stared at me for a few seconds before she spoke, and I wondered what she was thinking of or afraid to ask.

"I love you, Ellie. You've been a good friend to me."

Never in a million years would I have expected to hear such words from her.

"It's been my privilege, Maggie. Thank you. I love you, too. Your strength has amazed me since the moment I met you." I smiled and squeezed her hand. She squeezed back, tears in her eyes now. "I wish you peace in your journey, my friend; I will never forget you."

"Thank you, Ellie."

We sat in silence, and she closed her eyes once again. I closed mine too, feeling grateful our paths had crossed.

After a minute, I asked, "Do you have any other questions for me?"

"No," she said.

"Is there anything else you're worried about? Do you need to talk to anyone?" She shook her head. "Did my explanation help with your fears?" I hoped I had helped to reduce them.

"Yes, I understand better now. It does help to hear those things from you—I trust you. I know you would never bullshit me."

I laughed out loud. "No way would I ever attempt to bullshit you, Maggie. You, my friend, have a built-in bullshit meter. Nobody could ever bullshit you!" We both laughed, hands still clasped.

We heard the front door open; her sister was back. It was probably best since the conversation was beginning to exhaust Maggie. I gently placed the fentanyl patch on her upper arm. When I was done, I explained the manner in which Percocet could be crushed— between two spoons—to make it easier to swallow. By adding a quarter of a teaspoon of water, it could be pulled up into an oral syringe and slowly administered between Maggie's cheek and gums. Barb said she understood, while Maggie simply nodded. I suggested Maggie would likely need the liquid morphine too for any shortness of breath.

I told them I was going on to my next visit and said I could call later to check in. Maggie was already falling fast asleep, exhausted after pulling out all the stops to talk with me. She was relaxed and didn't need any more conversation. She had more important work to do. I bent down and kissed Maggie's forehead.

"I'll see you tomorrow. I hope you'll be peaceful tonight."

Weakly, and without opening her tired eyes, she responded, "Me too."

In the kitchen, I explained to Barb that the tiny 0.5 milliliters of liquid medicine would eventually become hard for Maggie to swallow. I suggested administering half the dose and then waiting five minutes to administer the other half, allowing it to begin to be absorbed into her cheek. Her sister said she understood. I told her she might start to hear the phlegm rumbling in Maggie's throat, and showed her which medication to use when it occurred and wrote down the instructions.

"Keep giving the Levsin every four hours; it usually works well to dry up the phlegm."

I made a tracking sheet for her to write down the doses and administration times. Barb and I talked in the kitchen about what an amazing woman Maggie was and how courageous she had been right up to the end. Her illness had been hard on the family; they often felt helpless since Maggie wouldn't let them assist her. I was glad Barb knew her well and understood forcing care on her now would not be respecting Maggie's wishes.

We agreed she had been an independent woman, and this time of her life was no different than any other. Maintaining her comfort and respecting her dignity were the most important things her sister could do for her now. I suggested checking in from the doorway frequently to see if Maggie looked comfortable.

I never wanted families to be alarmed by rapid, shallow breathing, or long breaks in breathing. I wanted them to expect changes and know how to medicate for them. The other common breathing pattern is called Cheyne-Stokes. It usually presents as three breaths, a long break, a deep breath in, and then the pattern repeats. I reminded Barb that breathing changes were expected and quite normal, I did not want her to worry when they occurred.

The most difficult end-of-life symptom to listen to and manage is phlegm in the throat. Some diseases cause greater amounts of phlegm to accumulate and make it harder to manage. Knowing what to expect can help caregivers feel more in control and confident. I alerted the families of all the possibilities in order to reduce their anxiety and increase their confidence as caregivers.

I offered Barb a hug before I left and told her she was doing a great job. Once I was in my car, a steady stream began to fall onto my lap and my car seat—a seat that had absorbed countless tears, over the years, for many wonderful people. I thought about how I would miss visiting Maggie. I would miss her keeping me on my toes. I would miss her wit and her fortitude. I was grateful she had allowed me into her life and to have been given the privilege of being her hospice nurse.

That evening, when I called to check in, Barb reported that Maggie had been sleeping comfortably all afternoon. I reminded Barb I was on call overnight, and if she needed anything to please call me. I told her I would be back in the morning. She thanked me for the support.

"I hope you can rest tonight, Barb."

I heard from several other families overnight, but no calls from Maggie's sister. In the morning, I made phone calls to check on patients and set up my day. With everything organized, I headed to Maggie's house, making it my first visit. When I entered, I immediately felt peace in the home. Barb seemed at ease too and said Maggie experienced some changes in her breathing, as we had discussed, but otherwise it was a quiet night.

"I thought she was gone a couple of times because she took such a long break in her breathing. But when I went to the door to look in, she would start breathing again." Barb reported.

"Yes, those breaks can seem like forever. Are you doing okay?"

"I didn't sleep very well; I stayed on the couch to be close. I'm okay, though, because she looks comfortable, and I'm thankful she's not in pain. I've been worried about how much pain she would have at the end," Barb admitted.

"I'm grateful she's comfortable too. Did you need to give much of the liquid morphine?"

"No. Since yesterday, she has only needed the morphine twice."

"The Levsin seems to be working I don't hear any phlegm."

"Yes, I've kept with it every six hours.

"Oh, that's good. Her comfort indicates that the fentanyl patch is working well. You're doing such a great job, Barb." Caregiving is such emotionally exhausting work, especially at times like these. Caregivers often need positive feedback to stay the course.

"Thanks. It feels good to finally be able to help my sister. She's been damn stubborn throughout this whole cancer diagnosis, rarely letting me do anything for her." We both smiled in appreciation of Maggie's strong spirit.

"Your ability to honor her wishes and let her do things her way was the greatest gift you could have given her."

Barb teared up—I knew it was hard for her to hear such things. The sisters were cut from the same cloth. I respected her need to be silent and decided it was a good time to leave her to her emotion.

"I'm going to check on her. I'll be back."

She nodded; I imagined she was unable to speak without the flood of emotion escaping.

When I entered the bedroom, Maggie was lying on her back. She was breathing in a deep and somewhat rapid pattern but did not appear uncomfortable. I assessed her heart rate at her wrist. I preferred the old-fashioned way of checking a pulse since it can tell you much more than a number from a machine can. It was rapid and thready (scarcely perceptible), at 132 beats per minute. It is not unusual at the end of life for the heart rate to become elevated, and peripheral pulses to become impalpable.

Her sister had placed a cool cloth on Maggie's forehead, as I had suggested the day before, to keep her more comfortable as her body pulled the heat to her core organs. This heat exchange is normal at the end of life. Many medical professionals and caregivers think patients are spiking a fever, when in fact they are working hard as a part of the dying process—holding energy in their core, leaving the extremities to cool down.

I often told families it seemed like some patients were running a marathon in those final hours, trying to get to the finish line as fast as they could. The heart rate goes up, their respirations become shallow and rapid, and most perspire heavily. Yet, amazingly, they do not appear uncomfortable; they are busy with the work of dying. No one else can do this important work for them. Keeping them comfortable with cool cloths, comfortable positions and medication during this part of the process is the best we, as caregivers, can offer.

Maggie looked otherwise comfortable to me, with no signs of pain, and this was gratifying. I knelt down next to the bed and reached for her hand.

"Maggie, it's Ellie. We're going to give you liquid morphine to try to relax your breathing a little bit; you're working very hard to breathe. Is that okay?" She nodded. "Are you in pain?"

"No."

Barb, standing in the doorway, heard my conversation and promptly brought in the liquid morphine. I used the small oral syringe to lace it between Maggie's cheek and gum. She was still able to swallow the dribbles I placed without choking. I gently flipped the washcloth over on her forehead, in order to give her the cool side

"Let me get a fresh one," Barb said. I heard the bathroom faucet, then Barb's phone ringing. In a muted tone, she began telling someone about Maggie's changes.

"It sounds like you had a restful night, Maggie. Are you still afraid?" I asked, noticing her eyes were half open and had the *looking-through-you-not-at-you,* appearance to them. This look told me the patient was not totally in this world or the next, but somewhere in between.

"No," she said.

I stroked her head across the crown, helping to move her vital energy.

"I'm glad, and I'm proud of you. You're doing great, Maggie."

As I watched her breathing, chest going up and down like a locomotive pushing the engine forward, I noticed she was not wearing the necklace with Jack's ashes. I had never seen her without it and remembered her description of its perfect placement—close to her heart.

I guessed Barb had taken it off when she bathed Maggie. I looked around the bedroom, glancing at the bedside tables, then noticed the necklace sitting atop the bureau. I got up to retrieve it, held it in the palm of my hand, and said a prayer for reconnection of the two soulmates. I knew it would be too much of a disruption to lift Maggie's head and put it around her neck again, so I placed it on her chest with my palm over her heart.

"Jack's right here, Maggie. He's with you. You are so close now; get on his back and ride away. Let your spirit be free. I wish you peace, my friend."

She managed a slight nod, as a single tear trickled down one cheek. There was sadness, knowing I would not see her alive again, and joy knowing, as she had hoped, she would soon be riding off free and wild—together again with Jack.

I sat quietly at the bedside, extending love and positive energy for Maggie to make her final journey. After about ten minutes, I went out to see her sister and told her Maggie was comfortable; her respirations had slowed, and her effort was much less labored since being given the morphine. I told her I had placed Jack above Maggie's heart and had asked her to ride away with him.

Barb began to cry. "Thank you for everything."

"You're welcome. Thank you for allowing me into your home, into these private spaces. I will never forget your sister. You've done such a great job of allowing her to maintain her independence and control. I know it was hard at times, but treating her with dignity was a true gift." I offered her a hug, and she accepted. I told her I was not a nurse, like some, who felt the need to predict the exact hour someone's life would end.

"Maggie could go at any time, but she will be the one to decide."

As I did with all families, I explained to Barb there was no rush to call hospice at the time of death.

"Take your time before you pick up the phone."

"Okay. I will."

"I'll let myself out."

Barb nodded and peeked into the bedroom for another look at her dying sister.

My next visit was two blocks away. No coincidence, I thought to myself, and very unusual, as my patient visits were usually several towns apart. About thirty-five minutes into the visit, my cell phone rang. It was Maggie's sister.

"Can you come back?"

"Yes, I'm on my way." Before I had a chance to ask, she had hung up.

I apologized to the family I was with, saying I needed to check on another patient. As with most hospice families, they were very understanding. Our visit was complete, and we were chatting as I input my documentation.

People understand a patient may be in crisis or a family may have lost their loved one and are in immediate need of a visit from the nurse. They recognize that one day they may be the one, on the other end of the phone, who needs the nurse right away. I appreciated their patience and understanding of the unpredictable nature of my workday.

As I drove to Maggie's house, I knew she would be gone, and I hoped her last moments had been comfortable. The door was open; I let myself in. Barb was in the kitchen, gathering up the medications for me to destroy.

With more composure than I expected, she said, "My sister

amazes me! I only checked on her once or twice after you left, and she was comfortable, her breathing steady. And then I was out here cleaning up and suddenly realized I didn't hear her breathing. I went in, and she was gone, just like that."

"I'm proud of her," I said, knowing it takes some courage to step away from this life. "And I'm glad for her and you that she went peacefully."

I approached her, and we shared a brief but tight hug, like teammates after a victory.

"Can I bathe Maggie and dress her in some of her favorite clothes before we call the funeral home?" I asked Barb.

"Of course."

She left the room and promptly returned with a nice comfortable pair of jeans and one of Maggie's favorite T-shirts fresh out of the dryer. I had seen her wear this T-shirt often. She had purchased it from a Navajo ranch and said the horse on it reminded her of Jack.

After Barb and I bathed Maggie, I placed the necklace with Jack's ashes around her neck. Now he was, as she had said, close to her heart where her soulmate belonged. I hoped they were riding joyfully together once again.

Maggie was a beautiful woman, and, even in death, she looked lovely and earthy. This was the last time I would see her. She wanted to be cremated and did not want any memorial services. Her sister told me the family planned to go out to dinner and share a toast to her life and her great, strong spirit.

During my years as Maggie's hospice nurse, I had learned many lessons about the benefits of allowing a patient to make his or her own choices. A great example of this was the day Maggie said she would rather feel short of breath once in a while and be able to continue to smoke than to have "damn oxygen tubing attached to my face all the time." Smoking calmed her, and she did not see any benefit in stopping. As she said, "I'm going to die anyway; I might just as well die doing the things that make me happy."

I loved her ability to choose her personal definition of quality of life. Thank you, Maggie, your lessons helped to make me a better hospice nurse.

11

THE MATRIARCH

Carol came home from a Boston hospital where she had almost died from side effects of chemotherapy and the overhydration that followed. This scenario was not something new to me. I had been on the receiving end of patients coming home from the hospital or oncology clinic in dire condition countless times. Most had heard the same message.

"There is nothing more we can do for you. It's time for you to have hospice."

Her family learned from the hospital staff Carol was only expected to live for a few days. She was being sent home to her daughter Diane's house and would be admitted to hospice services for her end-of-life care. Her daughter and son-in-law lived in a lovely home near the ocean, in a quiet neighborhood. Carol had a large family—a husband, several daughters and sons, and several grandchildren.

Her husband Mike and daughter Diane were in shock when I arrived at the home to admit Carol. She was minimally responsive as they rolled her from the ambulance into Diane's house. Her daughter said Carol had been in the same state for two days in the hospital intensive care unit (ICU). During the hospice intake process, the family told me stories about Carol's strength and determination throughout her cancer treatments.

It was clear Carol was the matriarch of the family. In her mid-sixties, she was a beautiful, youthful-looking woman, even with her silver hair. She had been living with a diagnosis of lung cancer for several years, presumably caused by many years of smoking.

At this stage, Carol had tumors scattered throughout both lungs; one tumor, in particular, was very large. These types of tumors cause fluid to build up in the space around the lungs and as the fluid level increases, so does the pain and inability to breath comfortably. A surgeon had inserted a tube that exited her body on the sidewall of her chest. This tube could drain the abundance of fluid through a vacuum system, a great option to keep patients comfortable in the home setting. A pressurized bottle is attached to the chest tube and, once the valve is released, the pressure in the bottle slowly pulls the fluid out. This procedure is generally only necessary every few days. The 500cc bottle can pull off roughly two cups of fluid.

The beauty of this device is that after the demonstration and instruction from a hospice nurse, most caregivers can independently perform the drainage. It is a painless procedure that improves patient comfort and breathing immediately. In Carol's case, we were removing between one-and-one-half to one-and-three-quarters cups of fluid each time. That may not sound like much, but in the small space surrounding a lung, this volume of fluid can greatly impede a patient's ability to breathe comfortably.

Carol was retaining fluid throughout the rest of her body as a result of intravenous (IV) hydration. Her arms, legs, and face were swollen and, according to her family, this was causing her significant discomfort. It was unsettling to see a patient in such a state of overhydration. I thought we might have time to pull off some of her fluid overload with medications and possibly extend her life by a few days or weeks.

I did not want to give the family false hope, so I simply suggested we could try to make her more comfortable by removing some of the fluid. They were in total agreement, wanting anything to improve her comfort. I had learned from past experience we had to work quickly to try to remove the fluid. Otherwise, the hospital prediction was right, and she would only survive for a few days, at best.

When I called the medical director to report the admission details, I included Carol's severe fluid overload. He and I had encountered this often over our years of hospice practice. We understood the hospital staff had been trying to correct Carol's dehydration and electrolyte imbalances by giving her the IV fluids. In the process, the additional fluid had shifted into all of the wrong places. This is called third-spacing. It means there is too much fluid for the circulatory system to hold. The only way it can manage the large volume is to push some fluid outside the blood vessels. This was the cause of the swelling in Carol's face, hands, feet, and abdomen. Third-spacing can cause other issues too. While the heart is doing its best to adjust to the changes, this shift can cause extremely low blood pressure and increased heart rate.

Carol exhibited all of these symptoms when I assessed her. The hospice medical director and I appreciated the opportunity to attempt to bring Carol back from the edge if we worked quickly. If we were successful, she might live a few weeks longer and die more comfortably. Comfort is always the goal of hospice care.

The medical director gave the orders for two different medicines, called diuretics; they help the body remove the fluid. Because Carol still had her urinary catheter in place, it was easy to see the results. Within just a few days, she looked dramatically different, and her discomfort decreased markedly too. I was visiting daily and was so pleased to see her becoming more alert and interactive with her family. They were a lively bunch!

She started asking to eat again, something she had stopped doing in the ICU. The volume of fluid coming from around her lung was enormous. Each time I watched the vacutainer bottle fill, I was surprised at how quickly the fluid had returned. The hospice medical director had written orders to drain as needed for comfort or at least every two days. At this point it was necessary to drain daily to maintain Carol's comfort and reduce her labored breathing.

The trust between Carol, her family, and me was growing as they witnessed her returning to them in that first week. They were not ready to let her go and said they were glad to have more time with her. They had been blindsided when the doctors and case managers waited until the last day or two of her hospital stay to tell them how close she was to death.

Many family members began to come to the home for brief visits to see Carol and say their goodbyes. She kept telling everyone she wasn't going anywhere just yet. She said her husband wasn't nearly ready, and she needed to "get some things in order." No one argued with Carol because they knew better. I was learning if anyone could defy the odds, it would be her.

Typically, there is one person a patient worries most about leaving. In this case, it was Carol's husband, Mike. She was worried because she didn't know how he would manage without her; he had begun to lean on her as he aged and hand off more responsibilities to her.

The plan was for Mike to continue living with his daughter and her family after Carol was gone. She said this plan reduced her worries and gave her comfort. I told Carol I would talk with Mike, to see how he was managing and then report back to her. She permitted me to do so. I suggested Mike would benefit from social worker and hospice chaplain visits. She agreed but was unsure whether he would accept their support.

I met with Mike privately in the kitchen. He had been relatively quiet during my visits thus far. He was a gentleman, very caring, and I could sense he was emotionally fragile. I offered to have the social worker and chaplain make visits to support him. Surprisingly, he was very open and agreeable to the suggestion. I immediately put out the referral calls to my colleagues. They both responded quickly and scheduled a visit with him within the week. Mike connected easily with both of them, seeing one or the other each week. As time went on, he said he looked forward to seeing them and appreciated their guidance. Carol was thankful they could support Mike. However, as a strong, independent woman, she continued to decline their offers to visit with her at any length. She was most interested in their updates about how Mike was doing.

As the weeks passed, Carol began getting out of bed more often and spending hours in the recliner in her bedroom. The volume of fluid on her lungs had decreased and now she could go two days without needing to have it drained for comfort. The medical director had reduced her diuretic doses after the large volumes of fluid had been successfully removed. Before too long, she was using her walker and moving slowly about the house. I was amazed by her ability to fight the disease that was waging war on her body. I followed her lead and continued to look for ways to increase her quality of life, for as long as we possibly could. Carol was not ready to die.

One day I suggested we remove the urinary catheter to see if she could begin to use the bathroom again. Something as simple as removing a catheter can restore some of a patient's independence. I had learned never to underestimate the power of that need. Patients would tell me they welcomed being given back some control of their life—an essential message for healthcare providers and family members. Sometimes, in our attempts to help care for patients, we forget to involve them in the decisions or activities they are still capable of performing—patient autonomy. Our efforts to provide care can become a disservice if we are not paying attention and listening to our patients.

Carol was surprised by my suggestion to remove the catheter, but she was more than willing to try. I removed it, and she immediately used her walker to get to the bathroom and attempted to use the toilet. Success! I wished I could have sent a snapshot of Carol to the ICU staff as she did her little victory dance in front of her walker when she returned from the bedroom. I imagined they would be shocked to learn she was still alive, adequately hydrated, and comfortable a full month after her discharge, never mind up and dancing.

Carol's little granddaughter, Lexi, was now spending a lot of time visiting. Most weeks she would arrive on Friday afternoon and stay until Sunday evening. The two had an extraordinary bond. Although she was only seven, she seemed like an old soul to me. She had a look indicating she knew too much, even though the family said no one had told her the details of her grandmother's situation. They had kept her away when Carol was at her worst, not wanting her to see her grandmother when she had been unresponsive. The family had been unsure of how to explain the situation to a seven-year-old, but I have learned young children seem to know more than we realize. Sometimes not telling them what is happening, in terms they can relate to, causes them to imagine something even scarier.

The love the little granddaughter received from her grandmother was constant and precious, safe and secure. Over Lexi's life, Carol had always covered any needs for her care whenever it was necessary. The special time they spent together had made Carol more like a mother than a grandmother to the child.

During my visits, Lexi would often sit next to me in the cozy recliner in Carol's bedroom. As I typed away on my laptop, she would ask what I was doing, and I would say I was writing a story about her grandmother. My response would make her smile and giggle. She would bounce away happily and then, after a few minutes, return to present me with a drawing. Lexi would tell me the pictures were for the story I was writing about her grandmother.

Sometimes she drew pictures of the two of them holding hands and doing things together. Other times the images depicted a little girl with flowers, sunshine, and rainbows all around her. Even in this situation, Lexi was a happy little girl, and her artwork was the evidence.

I had children in their teens and twenties, but no grown children who had given me grandchildren just yet. Witnessing this bond made me think of how wonderful it would be to have grandchildren of my own one day. It also broke my heart to imagine how this little child would feel when her rock, her source of unconditional love, left her life.

Carol was still alive two months after being sent home to die and had no plans to go anywhere soon. She and her daughter started discussing going out to one of her favorite stores to do some shopping once she was able. Although she was moving around the house, she tired easily and napped often.

Six weeks later, her strength and mobility had improved. Carol was asking more about when she and her daughter Diane could go on an outing. I suggested we order a transfer chair to reserve some of her energy when she went out on these adventures. Initially, in her independent way, she said she didn't want it; she wanted to walk on her own. I gently reminded her that her energy reserves were smaller than they used to be and using the transfer chair could allow her to be out longer. Additionally, I pointed out the risk of a fall was just not worth it after all she had gone through to get back to this place. She thanked me for the input and said she would discuss it with her daughter and let me know her decision at my next visit. I respected her need to think it over.

At my next visit, on a Wednesday, she asked me to order the transfer chair. I asked no questions, picked up my phone, and placed the order. It arrived the next day. Her daughter later told me Carol could hardly wait to get out and use it. Due to Diane's busy weekday work schedule, they had planned a Saturday outing. When I arrived on Monday, Carol was all smiles.

"How was your adventure?" I asked right away, curious about how it all went.

"I got you something." Carol beamed as she handed me the small gift bag.

"I'm not supposed to accept gifts, Carol," I responded.

Although the hospice agency had programmed the staff to say this, I had always been uncomfortable with it. I knew that families liked to offer a little token of appreciation for our support. In these small ways, it seemed appropriate—in my opinion anyway. So, I practiced my passive resistance to the hierarchy for the good of the patient and the value of human kindness. I smiled at her and reached for the bag.

"Oh, it's nothing, just open it," she said. I opened the bag and pulled out a little oblong stuffed toy with a tiny face and the words "Happy Pill" on its belly.

"Squeeze it!" she told me. I pressed the little pill and the giggles of a toddler erupted. We both started laughing at the joyful noise. I pressed it again.

"I love it, Carol, thank you!" I leaned down and hugged her as she sat in the recliner chair by her bed. She was one who appreciated a good hug hello and a hug goodbye at each visit.

"You're welcome. I thought of you right away when I saw it. You are like a happy pill for me, every time you visit!"

"You're too kind, Carol. I just love coming to see you and

your family. I'll think of you whenever I squeeze my Happy Pill and hear the laughter. Thank you so much for thinking of me."

I still have this precious, heartfelt gift she gave me on that day. I didn't have grandchildren at the time, but now, more than ten years later, I have been blessed with three of my own. How fitting my grandchildren play with the Happy Pill. When they press it, and it giggles, we laugh together. It's a beautiful reminder of Carol—the strength, love, and guidance she brought to her family and the lessons she taught me.

Carol continued to make short trips outside the home. She and her daughter made one outing to the store she had worked in for many years. It was said to have been a pleasant surprise for her coworkers to see her again, less than six months after they were told she was in a Boston hospital dying of severe complications from her cancer treatments.

One day I arrived to find her husband Mike up in arms and wanting to speak with me privately. He rarely asked to talk with me alone. In fact, Carol usually asked him to leave us alone when I visited to protect him from the details of her care and decline. On this day, he was angry with Carol. He pleaded with me to speak to her about sneaking cigarettes in the bathroom.

"It's the reason she's dying! Why would she want to smoke? I don't get it," he said to me in exasperation.

I don't think he expected the response I gave, but in these situations, I attempt to advocate for the patient first. I explained smoking is often a comfort measure for someone who has smoked, like Carol had, for so many years. I went on to say that although it may have caused her cancer, smoking at that point would not change her situation.

I understood his being upset but didn't feel I should tell her to stop. I assured him she would most likely get coughing pretty hard from it, and a few puffs would be all she could handle at one time. When I asked him to try to allow her control over the decision since she had lost control of most everything else, he began to cry. I offered him a hug, but he declined, saying he was fine. He was disappointed in me. I did promise to let Carol know how scary and upsetting her smoking was for him, and he said he would appreciate any effort on my part.

"She listens to you. Tell her not to smoke!"

"I understand you are upset by her smoking, but I can promise you it won't last more than a few weeks at best." I was thankful it didn't.

Carol could hear our distant voices and, when I entered her bedroom, she immediately asked what we were discussing. I admitted Mike had told me how she was sneaking into the bathroom to smoke cigarettes. I told her he was scared to think she would do this in her condition. Carol became teary and said she missed smoking because it had always calmed her when she was nervous or upset.

"Are you feeling anxious, Carol?" I asked.

"Yes. I'm having trouble sleeping. I wake up and just can't stop thinking."

"Do you want to talk about it with me? You don't have to, but I'm happy to listen and help if I can," I offered, in hopes that would get her through this tough phase.

"I'm starting to feel exhausted all the time again. I was doing so well, and maybe I started to believe I would live. But I know it's not true, and I just can't imagine leaving them. Do you see how I support everyone in this house? They rely on me for so much. How will they do it without me?"

She was teary again. I had not seen her in such a vulnerable state before. "Can I sit next to you on the bed, Carol?" I asked.

"Of course," she said, as she patted the bed.

I sat and pulled my feet up next to hers, then took her hand. Carol never hesitated to ask me tough questions or share private things about her family. I, in return, always kept those conversations in confidence.

She once told me she thought God had sent me as her special angel to pull her back from the brink of death, in order for her to have more time with her family. It made me cry a little to hear this. I was humbled by such a gracious thought, and grateful I had been able to extend her life with the help of the medical director. But I didn't feel like a special angel of sorts. I saw myself as a hospice nurse simply doing my job to the best of my ability. This meant working as a patient advocate and doing everything in my power to maintain the best quality of life for her. My work was rewarding and purposeful.

It made me uncomfortable to be put on a pedestal, as people often did with most hospice staff. Yet, I understood patients and families wanted to show their feelings and appreciation for the support we offered. I had learned to graciously accept the praise and appreciation—my mentor had taught me never to look for it.

As I settled in next to Carol, holding her hand, I mentally prepared myself for the bold and straightforward questions I knew would come from this courageous woman. She had never been one to beat around the bush. I took a deep breath, and she followed suit.

"Tell me what you're thinking and feeling, Carol, and I'll do my best to help." I listened intently as she began.

"First let me say, I'm not scared. I faced death in the hospital, and I have been well aware that it's coming. I don't know how I can ever repay you and the amazing hospice medical director for bringing me back. I looked like a grape when I came home!"

We both laughed, a little emotion choked back with the laughter.

"You sure did!" I said. "But in a few days, you were back to your beautiful self."

"I couldn't have imagined leaving all of them then. They

weren't prepared, and I wasn't ready to die. I hate to leave them now, but I am so tired ... I've worked hard to prepare them, and honestly, don't think I can do much more." She let out a small sigh of exhaustion.

"You're amazing, Carol. You've been so unselfish. You've shown an incredible ability to deal with your illness and all that comes with it. At the same time, you've supported your family during their emotional roller-coaster ride, not to mention managing the everyday busy life around here."

"I can't hang around and have them see me slowly fading away—it would be too hard for them," she said, with some fortitude.

"I agree. Can I share something I've learned from other dying patients?"

"Of course. I'm curious," she responded.

I took a deep breath and started in on a conversation I had shared with so many patients, each time not knowing how it would be received.

"Carol, I've learned that although we've been taught the heart or brain decides when we die by ceasing to function, or doctors and nurses can predict the time of death, none of it holds true." I waited for her to take it in.

"What do you mean?" she asked.

"Well, over the years, I've watched my patients choose their time. Many patients who physically and clinically shouldn't have been able to sustain life, somehow defied their bodies and lived long beyond what seemed possible—like you have—while other patients who had strong hearts said they were ready to die and died quickly. I have even had several patients tell me the exact day they thought they would die, and it proved to be true."

"That's incredible!"

"I think so, too. I believe the true experts on death are the dying. So, I have taken these lessons and shared them with many of my patients over the years. I hope it brings comfort to learn you have more control over the moment of death than you've been led to believe."

"You know what? It does. And now, thinking about it, I guess it doesn't surprise me. I had some dreams in the hospital about dying. In one dream, I told my deceased sister I wasn't ready to die, to come back for me later."

"I believe you, and I also think it wasn't a dream. Many of my patients have shared those dream-like states where they see and speak to a deceased loved one. There's more going on spiritually, in my opinion, than most of us realize."

"Yes, I agree. I have peace about dying. It's strange. I'm more worried about my family than I am about dying."

"This is common as well. Many patients are less worried about themselves at the end of life and tend to be more worried about their loved ones. They want to ensure their families are ready to let them go, sometimes even to the point of needing to have their permission to die."

"I just want to know they'll be okay when I'm not here," she said.

I nodded in understanding. "This is where trust comes in, Carol. You have to believe in them and trust they'll do the best they can without you. I'm sure life will never be the same here once you're gone, and I imagine they'll miss you tremendously, but I have a feeling they'll want to do their best for you in recognition of all you've given to them."

"Thank you. And it does help to hear what other patients have gone through." She squeezed my hand.

"You're welcome. Thank you for allowing me to care for you over these many months. I am so glad to have been your hospice nurse. I've learned a lot from you through your wisdom and bravery, Carol." She squeezed my hand firmly now before she dug into the tough question.

"So, tell me how it works when I'm dying. What will my family see?"

That's my friend, fearless and bold as ever, I thought. "Well, you have already started to prepare them in ways you may not be aware of." She looked a bit puzzled. "For example, you haven't been eating for a few days, just wanting liquids."

"That's true, I'm not interested in food anymore."

"It's normal at the end of life. I'm guessing we won't need food to feed our spirits on the other side," I said, smiling at her. She nodded and smiled back at me.

She pushed for more details. "What else?"

"Well, I've been told you've been sleeping most of the day and night and having fewer conversations with your family."

"Who told you this?" she asked.

"Diane and Mike." I waited to see how she would respond to their impression of her current state.

"What did they think about it? Tell me what they said, exactly." She appeared concerned.

"They were a little worried—as families often are—since you haven't been eating. They worry you will starve if you don't eat. I explained having liquids is fine because you are honoring the changes in your body. Forcing food at this time could cause some discomfort."

"Were they okay with this explanation?"

"Yes, they seemed to accept it, especially since they noticed you were sleeping most of the time anyway."

"I'm surprised, but relieved," she responded. "Maybe they'll do better than I think they will."

"Well, some of them have your genes!"

She laughed loudly, a twinkle in her blue eyes.

"You're damn right, they do!" she said proudly. I loved seeing her fierceness emerge.

I let the silence linger on this positive note before answering her primary question. I knew she wouldn't let me skip over it. "Let me answer your questions about what happens when you're dying. First of all, I promise you will always hear your family talking to you, even when you're too weak to speak. Patients are very busy in those final days and hours reviewing their life, laying things to rest in an attempt to find peace. Does this make sense to you?"

"I feel like I've already been doing that." She showed no discomfort about the subject matter.

"I think you have. It's probably why you said you don't feel afraid to die. I've learned from my patients, the more that's left unresolved in life and relationships, the more anxious they are about leaving. There's a lot of work to do. If you're having trouble sleeping, we can give you an Ativan tab at bedtime to help you relax."

"I'm going to start calling some of my relatives to say goodbye," she said matter-of-factly. She had moved on without responding to my offer.

"That's a great idea," I said, wondering if the conversation had helped ease the anxiety so there was no need for Ativan. Sometimes conversations are more powerful and healing than medicine—another great lesson I learned from patients. Let them share their fears; don't try to tell them medications alone can take them away.

"Okay, so what happens next?"

She's not done with me yet, I thought. "Well, during this phase, which we refer to as a *life review,* you appear to be asleep. We have learned patients are busy doing important and necessary work before death. We see patients reaching their arms out, having conversations with people we can't see. They frequently tell us they are talking to the deceased. Sometimes they ask questions of them about how to die, or say to them, not now, come back later. Often, patients talk about catching a bus, plane, or buying a ticket and having to go—all symbolisms for death. This is very common behavior."

"I experienced that in the hospital, didn't I?" she asked me, to be sure.

"Yes, according to your family, it sounds like you did. Maybe it was a practice run, so this time it will be easier for you since you've done some of the work already. Dying is hard work." I offered some encouragement for her efforts, in light of this little-known fact.

"No, kidding! It really is. Why the hell don't we learn more about it when we're alive?" she asked, with some of the toughness I loved about her.

"My personal opinion is people fear facing or accepting the idea of death. Somehow, I think they believe that by doing so, it will bring them closer to it. In reality, facing it allows us to live this life more freely and joyfully. At least, this is how it feels to me."

"Well, I faced it because I had to with this cancer diagnosis. I doubt I would have otherwise. It's tough to think about," she admitted.

I waited to see where she wanted to go next in our conversation.

"How long will it take for me to die?" she asked, point-blank.

"That's a tough question. I can tell you what your body goes through in the process, but how long, I believe, is in your hands."

Pushing forward, she said, "Okay, tell me about how my body will die."

I took a deep breath in preparation for the conversation we were about to embark upon, not my favorite to have with patients, but I always pushed forward out of respect for their wish to be informed.

"As I mentioned, you'll be aware of your family's presence.

You'll have a heightened awareness of time, people coming and going, and conversations taking place in the home."

"Really?"

"Yes, I've observed this. Frequently, patients will know about things before they happen, like unexpected visitors or conversations requiring their input. It's sometimes funny how they'll lie silent for days with the family sitting at their bedside talking. Suddenly the patient will chime in with a comment. It usually takes the family's breath away!"

"That's great. I like hearing this, thanks." She squeezed my hand again. I squeezed back.

"Go on."

"I'm glad this is helping you, Carol. You're so brave to ask all these questions."

"Well, I want to know what's going to happen to me and what my family will see. Go on," she said again.

"As you sleep more and become more relaxed, your breathing begins to change. At first, there might be a pause of ten to fifteen seconds or so, but then the pauses become longer, up to a minute for some people."

"Wow! That's a long time without breathing."

"It is. I call it practicing not needing to breathe. I'll prepare your family for this, so they don't get scared by it. It can sometimes be difficult for families to witness, mainly because breathing changes are frequently accompanied by the sound of phlegm beginning to accumulate in the upper airway." I don't enjoy sharing this fact, because I don't want my patients to worry about suffocating at the end of life.

"What do you mean?" she asked.

I tried to explain it in layman's terms as best I could. "As your body relaxes and the muscles in your chest follow suit, they no longer work to move the phlegm around like they normally would. So, it accumulates and makes a rumbling sound."

"Can't I just cough the phlegm up?"

"Usually, at this point, you are too relaxed and weak to cough it up. We have a couple of medications to dry up the phlegm. But I'll be honest with you; your lung disease is producing a lot of fluid. I may not be able to stop it completely. We'll continue to drain the fluid from your lung with the vacutainers, which will help," I added, hoping to ease any fear.

"Will I choke or struggle to breathe because of it?" she asked.

"Please don't worry. You won't choke to death on it, I promise. Patients don't seem to be bothered by this phlegm as much as the ones who are listening to it."

"Okay, I know you'll do what you can for me."

This trust patients and their families have for the hospice team is sacred and should be honored to the best of our ability. I tried to be worthy of it.

"Thank you, Carol. Your trust means a lot to me, and I promise I'll do my very best for you and your family. I know all of the hospice staff will." I wrapped my arm around her shoulder and hugged her.

"Will you be with me when I die?" She rested her head on my shoulder. I was glad she couldn't see my face while I pushed back the tears.

"I don't know if you will want or even need me here. It will happen in the way you choose. You may choose to have someone at your side or go privately when your family is asleep or out of the room ... I have no doubt you are going to do this just beautifully." I rested my head on hers, thinking about how much I would miss this incredible, strong, and beautiful woman when she was gone.

She broke the silence, lifted her head off my shoulder, and turned to look at me directly. "What happens after I die?"

Wow! That's my brave friend, I thought. "If I'm not here when you die, I'll come after your family calls hospice to tell us.

If it's in the middle of the night, the on-call nurse will come out to pronounce you. We'll give you a nice bath to freshen you up, put you in some clean clothes, and comb your beautiful hair." Our blue eyes locked as I smiled at her. She smiled and rested her head back on my shoulder.

"We'll make sure you go out looking beautiful and peaceful," I promised her.

"You know, I wasn't really afraid to die before we talked, but I'm glad I asked about how it works. I feel even better about it now," she said. "I have some calls to make." She motioned toward the bedside table. "Can you hand me the phone?"

I was relieved and happy to see the positive effect of our conversation. I handed her the cordless phone.

"Would you like me to leave so you can have privacy?" I asked.

"Heck no, I feel better doing this with you here. Sit in your usual spot over there and write your story about me. It's going to be a long one today, girl!"

I just love this woman, I thought, as I swung my legs off the bed and onto the floor. I sat in the recliner and pulled my laptop from my satchel. No vital signs were necessary today; I had much more intimate notes to write. I started typing while she called her siblings to say goodbye.

She was matter-of-fact with them. "I'm dying," she would say, then a pause as they responded. Then she would tell them, "I just know. I'm tired, and I can't do it anymore. I'm ready to die and wanted to say goodbye to you and tell you how much I love you. Oh, don't cry, come on. I should be the one crying. If I can be brave, so can you!"

This same conversation continued over several phone calls. I typed away, in awe of her. She had sustained many losses in her life—of parents, siblings, friends, even grandchildren. In all instances, she was reportedly the strength for everyone. Secretly, I did wonder how the family would manage without her. I imagined her family, especially her daughters and granddaughters, had the fighting spirit passed down from her to help them carry on and make her proud.

I had been typing for about fifteen minutes as she continued to make the brief calls. I could see she was getting tired when we heard a little knock at the door.

"Is it okay?" I asked.

"Yes. Come in," she called to the visitor, holding the phone to one side. Her precious little granddaughter and soulmate entered the room.

"Hi, Nana!" Lexi said, and went immediately to the bedside for her hug and kiss. She climbed up slowly, using the hospital bed rail, and gave her grandmother a gentle hug and a kiss. Then, seeing she was on the phone, Lexi climbed back down and came to snuggle up at my side, as was our ritual.

"Are you writing Nana's story?" she asked, her pretty blue eyes shining.

"I am. It's a long chapter today, Lexi," I told the precious little girl who possessed the same beautiful blue eyes as her grandmother.

"Should I draw a picture?" she asked.

"Yes! That would be so nice."

She bounced away. Carol said goodbye to one sibling and dialed another number, this time it was her sister, whom she was especially close to. I assumed she had been saving the toughest conversation for last. I don't think she noticed her granddaughter reentering the room with colored markers and paper in hand.

"I'm calling to tell you I'm dying," she said, this time with a bit more emotion and tearfulness than in the previous conversations. She didn't need to hold back for her sister; they knew each other too well.

The little girl's eyes grew bigger. She dropped the paper and markers on the floor, climbed into the chair, and curled herself into me. I hugged her tightly.

"I'm sorry, sweetheart," I said quietly. Her tears came, but she didn't speak. I couldn't stop the tears as they came to my own eyes. Lexi cried softly as I hugged her. It seemed she intuitively understood not to disrupt her grandmother's meaningful conversation. At that moment, I knew she indeed was her grandmother's soulmate. She was protective, loving, and courageous during the deepest despair. She had been given the very same strong qualities her grandmother possessed.

Carol kept the conversation short with her sister and let out a big sigh as she set the phone down on the bed—done at last. When she looked over at me, she noticed Lexi with her legs curled up, face buried under my arm, crying quietly.

"Come here, honey." Carol reached out her arms to her precious granddaughter. I lifted the little girl and carried her over to the bed.

"Shall I go so you can talk privately?" I asked.

"No, please stay. I think you can help."

I sat back down in the chair, wiping my own tears, wishing I could leave and let the huge emotion out, but knew being present for Carol was the most important thing I could do for her. I took some deep breaths to compose myself. Carol held the little girl tightly as Lexi sobbed and digested the thought of losing her grandmother. The scene was extremely moving.

At these moments, when I was so vulnerable, I sometimes wondered if I had any business being the one to support people through such incredibly personal moments in their lives. I would ask myself if I could maintain composure and offer the stabilizing force they needed. Somehow, the composure and the right words would come to me out of nowhere. It was beyond me and felt like a form of divine intervention and strength. I appreciated this guidance and relied heavily upon it to get me through the challenging places and spaces I shared with my patients and their families.

Carol snuggled her granddaughter to her chest and stroked her long blonde hair. "I love you so much, Lexi. I know it's sad for you to hear Nana say she is dying. But please don't be afraid, honey. It's time for Nana to go to heaven …" She stroked her hair again and kissed her forehead. "I'm exhausted, and my body isn't working for me anymore." The little girl's sobs became louder. "Sweetheart, I want you to remember how much you've helped me by visiting while I've been sick, and how you've always made me so happy. You and I are soulmates, remember?" The little girl nodded. "Remember what it means?" Carol asked.

Through tears and sobs the brave little girl spoke. "That we will always be together."

"That's right." Carol replied, trying to bring comfort to the tiny breaking heart.

Now my tears were falling fast. I couldn't stop the emotion driven by this moment of incredible love and compassion; I was witnessing the most essential and lasting conversation the two would ever share.

"When I am in heaven, I will be watching over you for all of your life. I will send you rainbows and sunny days. You will feel my love inside your heart, forever. Okay, sweetheart?" She continued to stroke Lexi's beautiful blond hair.

"But I will miss you, Nana," the little girl sobbed.

"I will miss you too, my love. I know this is hard. But you are a strong girl, and I know you will do great things in your life. I'm so proud of you already. I won't be far from you, Lexi. Even though you won't see me when I'm in heaven, I think you will feel me. You can talk to me in your prayers, too. I will send angels to watch over you," she promised, trying to comfort Lexi's precious, breaking heart.

"You will?" asked the little girl.

"Yes! How many angels do you think I should send?"

Lexi's watery blue eyes looked out the window for the answer. "Maybe three? One for Papa and Auntie too." Her compassion and strength shone through her sadness.

"I think you're right. I will ask God for three angels to watch over my family."

Silence fell over the room as the conversation seeped into these two precious souls. I felt gratefully invisible in the chair by the bedside. I was glad I didn't have to speak; my emotions were thick in my throat, somewhat like those nasty secretions I had told Carol about earlier. I feared clearing my throat would open the dam of tears waiting to flow freely. I wiped my cheeks then took a deep breath, resting my head on the back of the chair, trying to keep it all in. I gave thanks for the privilege of being present for such an intimate and profound conversation.

Although I had seen Carol's strength in action for months, I could not get over her eloquent words and presentation in such a difficult moment. Carol was a true matriarch in every sense of the word. Maybe this was a given, being the oldest in a large family.

She kissed her little granddaughter, and then attempting to keep things on a positive note asked, "Were you going to draw another picture for the story Ellie is writing about me today?"

"Yes." The little girl smiled.

"Okay, that's great. Can you do it at the kitchen table, for Nana?" she asked.

"Okay," Lexi agreed as she climbed down from the bed. I helped her pick up the markers and paper that, in her shock, she had let fall to the floor. When she stood up, she looked back at her grandmother and stared at her for a moment before leaving the room. Her grandmother was deep in thought, gazing out the bedroom window, and did not see the look which seemed to say, I miss you already, Nana.

Once Lexi was gone, Carol asked me to have her daughter and

husband join her, so she could tell them she had decided it was time for her to die. Her daughter and I had been having conversations about Carol's decline throughout the week. She was prepared for the news but still cried when her mom shared her immediate plan to die. Gathering her strength, she said she wished for her mom to find the peace she needed.

Diane had been the primary caregiver throughout the six months Carol had miraculously continued to live. She had been draining the fluid from her mother's lungs to relieve Carol's discomfort. She had helped to complete her mother's financial and organizational tasks as well—all while supporting her own family's needs and holding down a full-time job. She was her mother's daughter and had her mom's strength and courage.

The discussion was harder for Carol's husband Mike. He relied on her for so much emotional support that he became teary anytime there was mention of her dying. He had not prepared himself. Therapy sessions had been tried and helped him to relax to some degree, but they did not alleviate his concerns about living without Carol. He said going forward in life without her seemed an impossible task to him. Several times during her six months of care, Carol had told me of her daughter and son-in-law's promise to care for Mike in their home for the rest of his life. She said knowing this gave her immense comfort.

Diane and I left her parents alone to have their sad and heartbreaking conversation. I couldn't decide who it would be harder for—Mike hearing she had to go, or Carol knowing telling him would break his heart. After only a few minutes, Mike came into the kitchen with watery eyes and said Carol had asked for me to return to her bedroom. I offered him a hug and he accepted.

"I'm so sorry Mike. Carol has lived far beyond what anyone ever would have imagined. But she is tired of fighting now. We have to let her go. She's most worried about you. If you can tell her that you'll do your best to carry on without her, I think it might give her some peace."

"You do?"

"Yes, hearing it from you would mean more than anything."

"I'll talk with her later. I'm a mess right now. But I get it. She told me she worried about me getting along without her. I have Diane and her family; they'll help me."

"I know they will. I think deep down you're strong too, Mike. You wouldn't have chosen Carol if you were weak." I smiled at him.

"Yes, she's always been a force to be reckoned with." His tears flowed.

"I think you'll recognize your own strength after Carol is gone. It can be hard to feel it when you are in the presence of someone as confident and caring as Carol. She loved taking care of her family, and as wonderful as that is, it didn't allow you to figure some things out for yourselves. You'll figure out how to live without her and you will do it together."

"Thanks. You had better get in there or she'll have your hide, kid." He laughed through his tears.

"You're right." She didn't like to be kept waiting. "Hey Mike, thanks for letting me be here with her and all of you." I said. Seeing that my sentiments had caused him to cry again, I choked back my own tears and headed down the hallway.

"Is he okay?" Carol asked, as I shut the bedroom door.

"He's doing his best to take it in. He's strong Carol. He couldn't have spent his life with you otherwise. You have an amazing family and they're going to make you proud."

"I hope so, I'm exhausted after so many emotional conversations."

I offered her a hug. She accepted and held on for a long time.

"I'm sorry, Carol. What a tough day this has been for you. I can understand why you're so exhausted."

"I just want to sleep. I'm also having pain in my chest now. Can you drain me before you go?" she asked, referring to the fluid buildup around her lung, which was causing the pain.

"Of course." I began to gather the sterile dressing kit and vacutainer bottle at the bedside. "I'll visit you again tomorrow, okay?" I knew she would likely be asleep soon.

"I would appreciate it. I think they might need you more than I will tomorrow."

"I'm going to call the social worker and chaplain after I leave, so they can offer visits."

"Good idea."

"Would you like them to visit with you too, Carol?"

"You know I don't need to see them."

"I just wanted to make the offer again. Some people change their minds as they move closer to death."

"Since when am I 'some people'?" Her sassiness was still intact.

I let out a loud laugh. "I just love you, Carol! I'm going to miss your feistiness."

"I love you too, honey. Thanks for everything."

"It's been my privilege to know you. I won't forget you and your great spirit. I've learned a lot from you."

"You have the Happy Pill to remind you."

"Well that's true, but regardless, I could never forget you, Carol. You're a special person in my book." I leaned down and kissed her on the head.

"Thanks back at ya, doll." We laughed together for what would be the last time.

I drained the fluid with the vacutainer bottle. Then, I changed the sterile dressing over the area where the tube exited her body on her chest wall. Finally, I got her settled into a comfortable position in her hospital bed and covered her up; I gave her one last hug.

She was fast asleep within a minute. I stood next to the bed, watching her sleep for a few minutes longer, having my ritualistic silent conversation with a dying patient. I wished her peace, beautiful energy, and strength to surround her on her journey. It was a bittersweet day.

I knew Carol had worked hard, for six months, to defy her body, and I could only imagine how tired she had become in the process. I also knew there was something extraordinary and powerful about a patient saying she was ready to die. Carol's acceptance coupled with the honest conversations with her family would allow for greater peace.

Carol didn't talk much to her family after that day. She did as she had told everyone she would; she began her dying process. Within two days, the secretions were thick, as I had predicted. Still, her daughter and I were able to manage them even better than I had expected, as we fought the tumor burden's production of fluid. The combination of the vacutainer bottles and the medications worked reasonably well to dry up the phlegm.

I visited every day until she died, three days later. Shortly after her daughter had checked on her in the early morning hours, she quietly passed while her family slept. True to her independent nature, Carol died without anyone by her side.

At her funeral, letters written by each of her five grandchildren were read aloud. The lights at the church flickered as many times during the readings. The family said they knew it was Carol telling them she was okay. They said they were in awe of her strong spirit during her life and in the afterlife.

12

THE LONG GOODBYE

I was working near his home when Wil called me requesting my input on his current health situation. I offered to head right over.

"I would appreciate it if it's not putting you out," he said.

"Not at all. I'll see you in ten minutes."

I could hear the urgency in his voice and knew this was something important that needed my prompt attention. Wil was not a man who would ask for immediate support unless it was necessary. I cleared my schedule for the remainder of the afternoon.

My longtime friend, now in his mid-eighties, greeted me at the door with a hug and his great smile. Something was different about him; an uneasiness I had never seen in him before. Wil invited me into the living room and thanked me for coming so quickly. He seemed a bit on edge, almost anxious—an unusual state to find him in. He was a happy, easygoing person, who rarely showed upset of any kind. I sensed we were about to step into an unfamiliar place together, one I was not fully prepared for.

We sat on the couch in the living room. The house was quiet, as his wife, Doris, was out walking. He said he had hoped this would be the case, so we could talk openly and privately. I knew he had health issues, assumed this was the cause for his concern, and wondered what was happening to him.

Wil told me he was unsure of how to go forward after learning he would need dialysis to stay alive for any length of time. He wanted to know what the process entailed and how it would benefit him. He said the doctor hadn't shared much information about it, and that they would be going to an information session in a week to learn more. Doris, his son Tim, and his granddaughter Molly would attend with him, but he wanted someone he trusted to give him all the details before attending the informational meeting.

I began explaining the medical and technical process and how he would be attached to a machine that would clean his blood since his kidneys could no longer manage efficiently due to his stage-five kidney disease. I went on to explain that the process takes between four and five hours, generally three times a week. Wil thought about this information for a few minutes.

"This sounds like a burden for my family," he said. "I don't want to burden them physically or financially."

Knowing I had a background in herbalism, he asked if there were anything natural he could take to speed up the demise of his kidneys.

"Could I do this instead of dialysis?" he asked.

Although I had many hospice patients over the years ask for the "Black Pill," to which I answered, "There is no Black Pill," I was surprised by his question. I took a deep breath and contemplated my answer, as my teacher/my *Gandhi* had taught me to do many years before in such situations.

"I have no knowledge of an herbal supplement that would shut down your kidneys," I began, "and if there were such a thing, it would rob you of going through your dying process. I couldn't live with myself if I suggested or supported you in bypassing an important and spiritual part of life."

Wil looked straight at me, his gentle eyes reflecting the uneasiness I had heard when he called me.

"I don't intend to put you in a bad place. My concern is only for the financial burden of my care and the toll of the care on my family."

"I don't believe your family would consider supporting and caring for you a burden. I hear what you are saying, and knowing you as I do, I understand you are a caregiver by nature and trade and cannot imagine yourself in a position of being cared for. Am I close?" I asked, reaching for his hand.

"Yes. How long could it go on? My needing dialysis and care?"

"Initially, you may be well enough to maintain the independent state you're in now. But as your kidney disease progresses or your Alzheimer's becomes more evident, your daily needs will increase. I can't predict the timeline. There are too many factors that can change this, and every person with the same diseases would have a different trajectory."

"That makes sense, but can you even guess at the timeline?"

I squeezed his hand and gave him a gentle smile while attempting to fight back tears. No matter how many times I was asked "How long will it take for me to die?" or "What will it be like?" I struggled to answer. I couldn't separate my compassion and emotion from a straightforward answer. I understood the fear patients had of the unknown—an unknown that was holding them hostage. I knew too much about the truth of the matter and had learned it must be fed to people in small portions; or else they would either choke on the truth or choose to starve themselves of it altogether. Neither would help them find a peaceful way through what appeared to be an impossible impasse. Out of compassion, I answered cautiously.

"Can I share something I've learned over the years in my

work with the dying? They're the best teachers and I call them the experts," I said.

"Please do. I need something to hold on to, Ellie. I'm not afraid to die, but I don't know the best route to take to get there."

I let go of his hand and sat facing him on the couch. I took a deep breath, as I had been taught, hoping he would follow the lead. I was thankful he followed suit. Then we took one more deep breath to bring the angst down another notch.

"Okay. I can tell you've done a lot of thinking about this already, which has created even more questions, concerns, and anxiety for you. I imagine you've discovered through your own work that knowing our time of death could actually create more burden."

"I know that's true."

"We are accustomed to having control of our lives and being organized. Illness can tip our world upside down and make us feel it is spinning out of control." Wil nodded in agreement. "If we were aware of the date and time of our death, I believe we would live with even more anxiety and fear with every passing minute—almost like sitting next to a bomb and waiting for it to explode." I could see him contemplating this, so I paused to allow him to digest these thoughts.

"We would lose the ability to live in the moment and enjoy life if we placed more focus on the approaching end of our life and the unknowns that come with it. For most of us, organized daily living and control are our greatest distractions from the death we fear." I paused again.

I have been asked hundreds of times by patients and their families to reveal the secret answer to their question, *When?* and have tried to help people understand they know more about their own time of death than they realize.

"People have more control over the dying process and

moment of death than they can imagine. You know this to be true from your own work."

"I do," he said.

"Somehow, when you're facing it, you begin to question so much of what you understood to be true."

We stared out at the backyard, watching the birds, a favorite pastime of his and mine. After a few minutes, he took in a deep breath and slowly let it out.

"Thank you for coming by so quickly to talk with me. I trust your judgment and guidance so much. I hope you can be with me when I do come to the end of my life."

Fighting back the tears but letting my eyes water so the whole dam didn't break loose, I nodded. "I hope so too. It would be a privilege and a great honor."

We sat quietly in our emotion. We knew each other well and appreciated our special connection. I hoped, as he had, I could be with him at the end of his life. It would be a gift to be present as he made his way. Still, I accepted it was impossible to know how it would all play out, and where our lives would be when the time came.

The porch door opened and in she came, returning from her walk full of smiles and energy, dressed neatly in her spring jacket and sage-green pants. I brushed away the trickle of saltwater on my cheek.

"Hello, Ellie. How nice to see you. I didn't know you were coming," Doris said.

I got up to give her a hug and buy more time to push back my emotion before I looked her in the eye.

"Hello, Doris. So nice to see you. I was in the area." Without any mention of the conversation that had transpired, I jumped into a happy conversation of family updates. She offered me a cup of tea and invited me to do some catching up with them. I accepted. Wil's glances at me were thankful ones; he knew he could rely on me to keep our conversation safe, as I had never been one for gossip.

Before I left, Wil told me he would be in touch in the coming weeks. I told him to call sooner if he wanted to talk. We all hugged goodbye, as was our friendly practice.

Two weeks later, I received an email from Wil's daughter, Ellen, asking me to join in a family meeting. She said her dad had requested my presence. Again, I was honored and agreed to attend. Wil's retired primary care doctor and friend, Jan, was invited, as was a hospice physician friend of many years, Mac. Of course, Ellen, Doris, and his son Tim, as well as his niece Barb, and only granddaughter, Molly, were all planning to attend.

On the day of the meeting, I arrived to find a friendly and welcoming group, sharing hugs upon each arrival. We gathered in the living room in a circular fashion, a circle of love and caring, if there ever was one.

In his respectful and kind manner, Wil thanked us all for gathering on his behalf. He reviewed his diagnoses and said his Alzheimer's and end-stage kidney disease were both progressing, and decisions had to be made. He said he looked forward to the input from every one of us, saying he valued the different perspectives, personally and medically, we could offer him and his family. He said mostly he appreciated the meaningful and unique relationships we each shared with him.

Wil was clear and to the point in his presentation, stating with conviction that it was not his desire to be kept alive by machines. He said he was not inclined to start dialysis. Yet, in discussion with his family, he had come to realize they were not ready to let him die in the near future. He said while he could understand this, he felt strongly he didn't want to be a burden to them. He was unsure of how to remedy this divide.

He went on to say he had maintained a strong commitment to living a life with purpose and passion for the things and people he loved. His concern was how Alzheimer's would affect his ability to continue to live in this way. He also was concerned the dialysis would merely lengthen his life without assuring a strong measure of quality remained. And finally, all of this would burden his family in the process. He wanted guidance regarding medical choices from the three of us with medical backgrounds.

"Can I *try* dialysis? What would happen if I stop? How long can it extend life?" he asked.

His retired primary care doctor, Jan, discussed the answers to the questions he had posed.

"You can start and stop dialysis anytime. It's your choice," she told him in her gentle, non-judgmental manner.

"Depending on the status of the kidneys, the length of life after stopping dialysis can vary," she went on. "Dialysis can extend life for years in most cases. Still, starting is a personal decision."

Wil's hospice physician friend, Mac, began the conversation about scripting an advance directive, with guidelines regarding when to stop dialysis.

"What matters most to you in your everyday life?" he asked Wil.

The answer came quickly and with a smile.

"Conversing, like this, and being able to think deeply like I have done all of my life gives me great pleasure. Reading is also important to me. In other words, if I can't do these things, be engaged with my family, ponder, think critically and deeply, and read books, I would not want to merely exist."

Mac suggested the Alzheimer's would be responsible for deteriorating those pieces of Wil's quality of life; not so much the kidney disease. He encouraged Wil to think about the wording of his advance directive so his family would know when to stop dialysis.

"It sounds like you want to ensure the wording reflects the quality of life you expect," Mac said.

"Yes. that's exactly right."

"Am I wrong in saying you hope Doris and your family can come to terms with the reality of your limited life expectancy?"

"No, you have that right too," Wil said, looking toward Doris.

Mac offered to help Wil and his children, whom he had chosen to be his healthcare agents, write the details of how he wanted decisions to be made as his health changed and care needs increased. They appreciated the kind offer and agreed assistance would be welcomed.

I had been quiet thus far. I tried to gently interject the fact that it can be extremely difficult for families to stop the dialysis treatments. I explained that it is, in essence, like stopping life support. I had witnessed patients lose the ability to make decisions and have that responsibility fall upon the family. Even with advance directive guidance, families struggled with stopping dialysis treatments, never feeling quite ready to let their loved one go.

Doris finally spoke. "We have to convince him to do the treatments." She was overtaken by emotion and it was all she could do to get that out before choking back sobs.

Ellen said she wanted to speak on behalf of the family about how they were feeling and what they were thinking. She too talked through choked-back tears. She said the family still saw Wil enjoying life and being engaged with family on a daily basis.

"We're all committed to helping with your care and healthcare decision-making. We don't see this as a burden, but more as a loving gesture to a man who is the respected patriarch of our family. Imagining life without your love and guidance is impossible for us at this point. We are requesting more time to prepare, not asking you to suffer for us, Papa. Dialysis could offer us that time."

Wil's son Tim saw his sister's emotion. "Dad, Ellen and I are here for you and Mom. We'll support you in whatever you decide is best for you." His own feelings stopped him there.

Wil was listening, and I knew, though he appreciated the input, he was not hearing what he had hoped to hear.

"I hoped there were some way to speed this up so all of you wouldn't have to be dragged along with me," Wil said.

"Oh Papa, please don't think of it that way," Ellen pleaded.

"We can handle this, Dad," Tim added.

I was thinking about the wisdom of Wil's thought process, questions, and foresight, especially in light of his Alzheimer's. The intention of being a caregiver is a heartfelt one by most. Yet, the lack of firsthand knowledge about the reality of the caregiver role is what often makes people so agreeable at the onset. If they understood the depth of exhaustion, emotional drain, and stress of the role, some would likely never agree to it. Still, most caregivers reported, all things considered, it can be a gift to be a caregiver.

As patients' needs increased, families would often report feeling the burden and guilt that accompanied it. I would tell them that when their loved ones were gone, they would have the lasting gift of knowing all they had done to make the last chapter at home possible. When they were in the center of the storm offering the care, a time warp in many ways, it was nearly impossible to have such perspective.

Wil, over his many years of spiritual work, had seen the reality of this burden on caregivers—both emotionally and physically—take its toll, sometimes even resulting in illness for an elderly caregiver. I understood the combination of this reality and a sincere love for his family was why Wil would have preferred to make his journey brief. There was no cowardly nature at work here, or fear of pain and suffering. He had been present at the bedside, all too often, of those who were suffering, and had prayed and assisted many to find peace in those times. He did not fear death—he accepted it as a part of life. He had thought about his own death during his lifetime; as a means of acceptance and preparation, he had attended and led vision quests in Death Valley. He was a willing participant in the journey, an unusual mindset I rarely encountered.

"May I share my perspective?" I asked.

Wil nodded. "Please do."

"I appreciate being asked into this sacred circle. I can see the difficult position each family member is in, and I recognize the emotional aspect of trying to imagine saying goodbye to Wil. I can also understand his worry about burdening the family in the process. Yet, the importance of making the journey to the end of his life, what it will teach him and all of you along the way, must not be overlooked."

As a minister of many years, Wil knew this to be true. "Yes, I know there is value in the process. I don't fear it or intend to avoid it. I hope we can come to a place where my family and I are all comfortable with the plan." The room was quiet, maybe uncomfortably so for a moment. All the questions posed by Wil had been answered, advance directives addressed, and family members had shared their feelings.

Wil, looking exhausted, closed the meeting. "Thank you all for coming today and for giving me your support and valuable input. I appreciate and love all of you."

"Thanks for asking us," Jan said, speaking for all.

Doris got up and said she would put the kettle on. The rest of the group was mingling and talking amongst themselves. I looked at my friend sitting quietly, taking it all in.

I approached him and sat in the now empty chair next to him.

"How do you think this went?" I asked.

"I think we got some good work accomplished. It was different than I had expected, but it's okay," he conceded.

I knew Wil well and recognized his unselfish manner and generous heart at work.

"Are you sure it's what you want?"

"Not totally." He smiled. "But it's a compromise I am willing to accept."

"I suppose that's what really matters, isn't it? I'm here for you, Wil."

"Yes, I know you are. Thank you for coming today."

"It was my privilege to be asked. I hope my insight was helpful."

"It was. I agree the journey has great value."

"Can I give you a hug?" I asked my dear friend.

"Absolutely, I could use one."

Two weeks later Wil started dialysis treatments. His appointments were early in the morning, so he and Doris had to rise at four in order for him to be there by six. They lived in a wonderful neighborhood where some of the neighbors had volunteered to be his drivers. This allowed Doris time to take her walk, prepare lunch, and not worry about the details of transport. This generous support was especially helpful during the winter months.

I visited from time to time and could see the decline in Wil's health, but was amazed by both his and Doris's ability to adapt. One day, after nine months of treatments, Wil fell coming into the house, sustaining compression fractures that went undiscovered for two months. Shortly thereafter, Doris fell and broke her humerus. The break made it challenging for her to be a caregiver and eventually the family realized it was too much for her to get Wil dressed, make breakfast, and get him out the door on time for his treatments, never mind keep up with the house.

Together with Tim and Ellen, Wil and Doris made the tough decision to move into an independent apartment in an assisted living community. This meant they had to sell their house and the kids were given the huge task of cleaning it out before putting it on the market. Tim lived locally and visited his parents several times a week; he would pick away at the task during each visit. Ellen came for long weekends to help them.

When the day came the move went well, and Wil and Doris slowly adjusted to their apartment life. It took time to adjust to the new way of living and socializing, and the distance from longtime friends, but they made the best of it. Their kind friends from their old neighborhood remained involved in Wil's transport to dialysis each week.

After more than two years of treatments and the continued progression of his dementia, Wil started becoming restless during dialysis. He could not be left alone for long during the treatments because he had started pulling on the catheter. I recognized this behavior as his message to stop dialysis, but the family was not ready to see it that way.

Doris began sitting with Wil, arriving at the clinic just before his treatment, but after a month it became too much for Doris to stay with Wil three days each week, for four to five hours, to keep him safe. His needs were changing, and it was becoming a challenge for Tim and Ellen to support their parents from a distance—especially with their own busy lives. That was when the family reached out to me. They wanted to hire me as their private duty nurse for support and to accompany Wil during two of his three weekly treatments and then transport him home afterward. His long-term care insurance would reimburse them for the cost of my visits, so it was a financially feasible plan.

Wil's former neighbors would continue to drop him off at the treatments in the morning. I would arrive after the nurses had time to get him weighed in and hooked up to the dialysis machine. I enjoyed being able to sit with my old friend. He knew me, and I still offered familiarity and comfort to him, but he rarely used my name any longer. It was obvious he had begun to have name retrieval challenges.

Although our discussions were no longer the same deep discussions of past years, we still laughed and found much to talk about. The time at dialysis went by swiftly, and he often talked to me about wanting to stop his treatments. I would relay this to Doris and the children, but they would encourage him to continue and he would reluctantly agree.

He now lacked the capacity to make decisions for himself. This had been determined by his physician, who had activated Wil's healthcare directive. I had talked to Tim and Ellen about the difficulty of being the healthcare agents and decision-makers for their dad. This position is especially challenging when the patient is on dialysis. Stopping meant he would live, at best, only a week or two afterward. This is an extremely heart-wrenching decision. Families in a similar circumstance had told me it seemed as if they were "pulling the plug" on their loved one's life. Of course, this is not the case, but this was their sentiment.

Even though this discussion had been part of the planning meeting and entered into his advance directive more than two years earlier, it was totally different to face it head-on. In truth, it had been discussed, acknowledged, and set aside until it weighed on them like a heavy boulder. My heart went out to the families who faced this dilemma. The one blessing in this situation was, even with his dementia, Wil was clearly asking to stop treatments.

One day, around five a.m., my phone rang. It was Ellen calling to say her mom had called her in a panic. Apparently, Doris woke to find Wil had been pulling on the catheter and had caused bleeding around it. Ellen said the catheter was still in place and the bleeding had stopped, but she wanted me to make a visit to her parents' home. I asked if they had discussed going to the hospital. She said they had, and thought since the catheter was not pulled out, and the bleeding had stopped, they didn't want to put Wil through the trauma of that process. I agreed to go, stating that if it were more than a simple dressing change, I would let her know and call the ambulance. She agreed to my plan.

I dressed quickly and headed out, driving down the stretch of highway between my home and theirs. It was still dark outside and few cars were on the road at that early hour, so there were no slowdowns to contend with. I called Doris when I arrived so she could let me in the locked exterior door.

"Come in," she said, motioning to me. We made our way up the short flight of stairs and into the apartment.

As I took off my coat, she went into the bedroom to be with Wil. When I entered the room, there were the two of them sitting up next to each other on the bed, Doris's hand pressed over a bloody washcloth covering the catheter. To my surprise, they were both smiling.

"Thank you so much for coming, Ellie. I didn't know what to do. I didn't want to call the ambulance and have him go to the hospital," Doris said. I could see she was nervous.

"I'm glad Ellen called me," I said as I set my bag down and unzipped the pocket with my hand sanitizer, rubbing it in thoroughly, then placing my exam gloves. I approached the bed and the bloody mess; Doris got up and stepped aside to let me in.

"Okay. Let's see what we have here. Are you having any pain?" I asked Wil as I removed the washcloth from his chest to get a closer look at the situation.

"No. No, pain," he said.

"Are you feeling dizzy or nauseated?"

"No," he responded. "I feel okay."

"That's good. I'm glad," I said, pleased to find him so calm.

"Would you mind bringing in some water or juice for him to sip while I get this cleaned up?" I asked Doris, knowing she would feel better keeping busy and allowing me to take a closer look.

"Sure," Doris replied, and she was off to the kitchen.

While she was gone, I assessed the catheter; no sutures had dislodged from his skin, and all were still well intact. I was relieved. It appeared he had been scratching around the area and caused some irritation and bleeding to the skin. The surrounding tissue needed a good cleaning with soap and water and then some betadine, followed by a new dressing. I had everything I needed to clean it and redress it in my nursing bag.

Doris returned with a small glass of cranberry juice, and I moved to the side.

"Here you go, dear," she said, handing him the glass.

"I'm going to fill the washbasin with water so I can get you cleaned up," I said to Wil.

"I can get one for you." Doris was out the door before I could respond.

She retrieved the washbasin, filled it with warm soapy water, and grabbed two clean wash cloths. She was speedy and efficient. When she returned to the bedroom, she set them on the bedside table. Wil was sipping on his juice and I was assembling the clean dressing materials on a clean paper chuck (disposable underpad) at the bedside.

"I think the best thing to do is to cut the T-shirt off and throw it away. It's probably too stained to keep. What do you think?" I asked.

"Yes," Doris agreed. "Do you need scissors?"

"No, I have my medical scissors. Would you mind getting them from the zipper pocket on the left side of my bag?" I asked, not wanting to take off my gloves.

She retrieved them for me and placed them on the paper chuck. I sat on the bed next to Wil, then smiled at both of them before I began.

"Thank you. You're a good scrub nurse," I said to Doris, hoping to help her relax a bit.

She laughed and shrugged her shoulders. "Oh, I don't know about that," she said.

"Well, I appreciate the help."

Then I turned to Wil. "This won't hurt," I explained to him before beginning. "I'm going to cut your T-shirt off."

"Okay. Cut away," he said with his usual positive attitude, no concern on his part.

I cut straight down from the neck to bottom of the shirt and then up each sleeve to the collar. Wil sat up and the T-shirt fell off easily. Doris took the blood-stained garment away, placing it in a small bag. I washed Wil's bloody arm and chest, rinsing and wringing the washcloth often. As I worked, I talked with them about another idea for keeping the catheter covered, suggesting this would make it harder for him to access the area. It took a few changes of the water in the basin before I was done and ready to cover the catheter.

I devised a dressing using a high absorbency pad with wide Kerlix tape to hold the large dressing firmly in place. Kerlix tape is kind on the skin and in conjunction with the skin prep I used to help it adhere better, it appeared to be a good choice in this situation. Afterward, I explained that itchiness was a common side effect of end-stage kidney disease. I told them I would call the doctor at the dialysis clinic to tell them what had happened and request medication for the itching.

After I had finished placing the dressing, I helped Wil into a clean T-shirt. Doris and Wil invited me to stay for breakfast and I happily agreed; it was almost seven a.m. by then. I helped Wil out of bed and he slowly made his way to the kitchen table, surfing the furniture, and sat down in anticipation of their usual breakfast. I went to work reorganizing my nursing bag in the adjoining living room. I noticed Doris was balancing on one foot at a time next to the kitchen counter, while the oatmeal cooked. Out of curiosity, I asked her what she was doing.

"This is my five-minute yoga workout routine. I do this every morning. Since it takes the same amount of time to cook breakfast, I can kill two birds with one stone." She snapped her fingers in the air and smiled.

"I love your idea. You don't waste a minute, do you, Doris?" I laughed.

In fact, I took a page from her book and began to do some stretching at my kitchen counter each morning while my coffee brewed.

After our breakfast, I called the dialysis clinic to inform them of the incident and the itching Wil was experiencing. They agreed to add the order for Benadryl to his medication list but said they could not dress the area after each treatment, not in the way I had, since they didn't stock such supplies. I was disappointed but understood. Even so, I knew it needed to be done in order to protect the catheter. So, after I got off the phone, I explained to the two of them that I would come to their apartment and dress the area after every treatment. Even on the one day I did not accompany him, I would still come to place the dressing to protect the catheter. They said they were grateful for my efforts, and I could immediately see the relief on Doris's face. Satisfied I had done all I could for the moment, I said my goodbyes, reminding them to swing by the pharmacy to pick up the Benadryl.

"We'll go by this morning," Doris assured me.

Once back home, I called Ellen to update her on what had transpired during my visit. She lived more than three hours away and said having me available 24/7 for a crisis gave her peace of mind. I understood how scary it must have been for her to get the five a.m. panicked phone call from her mom. This phone call opened an opportunity for discussion of the increased needs her parents were beginning to exhibit. She said she was trying to rearrange her work schedule to allow her some longer visits with them. Tim had been joining his parents for dinner once a week for years, but in recent months had increased his visits and had begun helping with filling the medication planner each week. Ellen and Tim kept in close contact and spoke on the phone about their parents' changing needs and their dad's decline but had no discussions about stopping the treatments.

I decided I should once again broach the subject of stopping dialysis.

"I think your dad is exhibiting more signs of discomfort and growing weary of the treatments. Without exception, every time I accompany him he tells me he wants to stop them," I said, knowing the message would be tough for her to hear, but wanting to advocate for my friend's choices.

"This is so hard, Ellie. I know he doesn't like the treatments … but I see him engaging and enjoying life when we are together."

I listened, allowing her to elaborate and not wanting to make any suggestion. One of the great lessons I had learned from my mentor and teacher—my *Gandhi*—was listen.

"I don't feel it is time to stop them."

I remained quiet, holding back any judgment, knowing the reality of the great divide she faced.

"He said as long as he was experiencing joy in his life he wanted to continue to live."

"He did," I agreed. I had witnessed him laughing, singing, and thoroughly enjoying his meals at every home visit. I could not deny this fact. But I knew the decision had to be made soon. I didn't want a crisis to take him out of this world. I hoped planning could offer him a peaceful death at home with his family by his side.

I had been a witness to this terrible dilemma too often, but never so connected to the people involved. As Wil's nurse, I was making my best effort to support and advocate for his wishes—

wishes he had clearly spelled out in a five-page narrative advance directive. This document was the result of his well-planned and purposeful meeting, almost two and a half years earlier, with friends and family whom he trusted to guide and support him. He had clearly lived much longer than any of us, most especially he, had expected.

I was also attempting to support the family and not push them in any specific direction. I had learned from past experience a good advocate must accept the choices the patient-chosen healthcare agent makes. In these situations, it is not my place to modify the plan unless asked for such input.

This is one reason choosing an appropriate healthcare agent is extremely important and can be so challenging. At first thought, it seems straightforward—pick a family member, since it obviously wouldn't make sense to put someone from outside your circle into this vital role. It's a role that comes with many challenges beyond the obvious responsibilities. In a utopian world, patients would choose someone who would follow their directives in a diplomatic way, without being swayed by others if push came to shove. In my experience, this is rarely the case.

Usually patients pick their spouse or eldest child to be their healthcare agent. When choosing the eldest child, many worry about offending their other children. I can count on one hand the number of patients who told me they chose their healthcare agent solely because they knew that person would honor their choices.

Often the person chosen faces pushback from loved ones when attempting to follow the patient's advance directive. It's common for families to have varied beliefs about what's best at any given time, especially with an unpredictable trajectory. I've witnessed huge blowouts amongst families who could not agree on what was best. Even when the patient was giving their input about wanting to stop living, loved ones (and sometimes healthcare providers) often urged them not to "give up."

When asked for my input in these instances, I went back to what the patient had spelled out in their healthcare directive. This could make me unpopular with someone in the group, but one doesn't become an advocate in order to make more friends or woo the crowd. I had learned you needed to have confidence and thick skin to succeed in this role.

It was certainly understandable that families were rarely ready to say goodbye to the person they loved, but I hoped the patients would not endure tremendous suffering as they waited for loved ones to let them go. Sadly, witnessing a loved one in pain was often the driving force behind family decisions to let it all come to an end. No one wants to see someone they love suffering. In these cases, it was necessary to increase pain medications, which generally had a side effect of drowsiness. This state sometimes allowed the families greater acceptance of the impending death as their interactions with their loved one decreased. According to most reports from families, being able to see them sleeping peacefully and out of pain was a welcome sight.

I left Ellen to mull over her thoughts about what was best for her dad. She said she planned to call Tim and discuss it further with him once she got off the phone with me. After the early morning incident, Ellen and Tim began visiting more to support their parents.

I visited two days later since we had increased my visits to three times a week in order to change the dressings. The new dressing plan was working well, as I had hoped. During my subsequent visits, I attempted to have more discussions about Wil's decline with Doris and the kids when they were present. Anytime I broached the subject Doris became annoyed with me. I was walking a tightrope between honoring him and supporting her.

Even though Wil was using a walker, I could see walking was becoming more of a challenge and worried about him falling. He had a small open area on one foot, and this was increasing in size and causing more discomfort when he walked long distances. A nurse from the local Visiting Nurse Association (VNA) had been coming into the home in recent weeks and she had been managing the wound. When Wil began complaining about it, she suggested a wound clinic visit might be in order. Additionally, I suggested that a transport chair would help get him get safely and comfortably out to the car and in and out of the clinic. Doris was not ready for this level of acceptance. To complicate matters, a physical therapist was coming from the VNA, twice a week. He was encouraging regular movement with a walker, saying Wil's mobility would increase his strength. The different viewpoints were confusing for the family.

I understand the optimism of physical therapists and have respect for their amazing abilities. They are wonderful at helping people regain their strength in the worst of circumstances. Unfortunately, this makes it difficult for them to recognize the signs of a true end-of-life decline that hospice nurses have had to learn to decipher. At certain points, patients can no longer safely ambulate long distances, even with a walker. Sometimes, strength can be maintained on flat surfaces, in small areas, with repetition.

I frequently encountered caregivers and medical providers who believed that if patients could move more, eat more, and be more positive, they would surely improve. This may be true to a degree but, at a certain point, it is called hope and can be unrealistic. Wil was at this point, and I worried about how to go forward without alienating his caregivers while advocating for my patient and longtime friend's safety. I was not judging their choices; this would not benefit anyone. I was applying years of firsthand experience to the situation. It upsets me to think of how many hospice patients, mine and my colleagues, sustained falls shortly before they died. Some of these falls caused major injuries, like hip fractures, which accelerated their deaths.

Allowing the family dynamics to play out in their usual fashion can be challenging for healthcare teams. Not getting stuck in the middle of them is a greater challenge. Wil's family had discussed everything in a planned and thoughtful way. Family meetings were a regular occurrence and allowed everyone to share their thoughts. These family gatherings became invaluable as time went on. Sometimes Ellen was on speakerphone during the meetings, while Tim and his parents gathered in the living room. Afterward, Ellen would email or call me with the details, to keep me in the loop.

After witnessing Wil's pain increasing, I strongly encouraged the family to obtain a transport wheelchair and start using it for long distances to maintain Wil's comfort and safety. I explained that falls are accidents, unplanned, and can be game changers. After some private family discussion, they did get one, and Tim had it delivered within a day—it sat folded up in the corner of the bedroom. I encouraged the use of it at each visit, but to no avail.

The wound care clinic visit started the process for getting a long-acting pain medication for Wil. I called Wil's primary care doctor to schedule a visit for the discussion. Initially, Wil agreed, but when I arrived the next day to take him, he was against it, stating, "I don't want all this medical process anymore." I called the doctor's office and rescheduled the appointment, hoping for Wil's agreement the following day. After telling Wil I had moved the visit to the next day to allow him time to think about it, he asked to be left alone, and sat in his chair in the bedroom meditating for two hours. I knew from our years of friendship this was a common practice that allowed him to connect to an inner peace. It was a practice he had told me was essential for him.

In the middle of the night, Doris got up to use the bathroom and found Wil wandering the hallway outside the apartment, looking for the "way out." She guided him back to bed and the next morning called Ellen to report his pain was high, and he had agreed to go to his doctor. I arrived in the mid-afternoon to transport and accompany them to the appointment.

Wil's primary doctor took his time listening and talking to them, asking Wil questions about his dialysis. When he understood Wil was ready to stop his treatments, he helped Doris come to terms with the end-of-life plan. He suggested end-of-life care be started soon after treatments stopped. Doris said she would rather not have all the new faces from hospice coming into their home. She told the doctor she and Wil planned to use my support and that of her children instead. But they had not set a stop date for the dialysis just yet.

The doctor said he understood and respected their choice. He told me he would give me his cell phone number so I would have direct access to him 24/7 for any necessary support and medication needs, once Wil was ready to stop dialysis. We discussed the comfort medications that are kept in the home for patients at the end of life, and he wrote the orders for them. Instead of liquid morphine, oxycodone, which is better tolerated by renal disease patients, was chosen. The medical staff called the medication orders into the local pharmacy, so we would have them in the home that afternoon. Finally, the doctor asked his office social worker to complete the Do Not Resuscitate (DNR) form during our visit and he signed it so we could post it in the home immediately. I was impressed with his thoroughness and compassion for Wil and Doris.

Once I had Wil and Doris settled back in at home, I went to pick up the medications. When I returned to the apartment, I showed Doris how and where to place the fentanyl patch. Next, I noted the time on the calendar, so we could change it in three days, at the same time. Wil and Doris were both exhausted by the medical visit and chose to have dinner and head right to bed afterward.

When I visited the next day, Wil's comfort was much

improved. I had warned he might be drowsy for the first day or two while he adjusted to the medication, but he was only mildly drowsy. I was thankful. I accompanied him to his treatments the next week. He talked more and more about needing to "be done with this." The man who should not have been able to articulate these thoughts due to the progression of his Alzheimer's was clearly sharing how he felt and what he wanted and didn't want.

Once we returned home after his treatments, I would share these conversations with Doris. She didn't want to enter into any discussion about stopping treatments anytime soon, and I could sense she continued to be annoyed with me for broaching the subject. I had been in the position of the unwelcome messenger many times over the years as I advocated for my hospice patients. I was stuck between a rock and hard place in my attempt to advocate for Wil without totally losing Doris's trust.

It is a tough position to be in for sure. You are attempting to honor what the patient is requesting, while at the same time trying not to alienate or lose the confidence of the caregivers you need to work closely with until the patient passes. Sometimes there is no easy way to accomplish this.

Ellen was more open to the discussion and said she would speak with her brother and they would try to talk with their mom about choosing a stop date for their dad's treatments. I tried to support Ellen as she struggled to enjoy time with him while attempting to prepare for saying goodbye. The family knew once the dialysis was stopped their time with Wil would be only days, generally two weeks at best.

Ellen, Tim, and their parents enjoyed listening to their favorite CDs and singing together. I loved being with them on these occasions. I saw my old friend in his true spirit as he smiled and tapped his foot to the music. There was one CD in particular they played over and over. It had become quite familiar to me as well, so soon enough I joined their choir. We had some wonderful afternoons together laughing and singing. Alzheimer's patients often respond with incredible clarity to music—it is a precious way to bring them back to you briefly.

Sometimes in their heart-to-heart talks, Wil would tell Ellen he was preparing to say goodbye. She would listen to his thoughts and ask him questions about whether there were things she and Tim needed to do for him to help him prepare. He was quite joyful in these discussions. She told me during one visit her dad said to her, "I have to go now. I'm looking for a door." She asked if she could help him find the door and they walked down the hallway outside the apartment—no doors along the way appealed to him.

When they returned to the apartment he said, "You know, I'm not afraid of death; I'm curious. I'm looking forward to this next chapter." Then, after a few minutes of pondering, he smiled at her.

"Okay, I have to go now. Toodle-oo!" he said in his playful fashion, then leaned over and gave her a kiss on the cheek.

The next morning Ellen and Doris took Wil to his dialysis treatment. Ellen sat with him while Doris went back home to take her morning walk and then relax; the changes in Wil were affecting her energy level too. When I arrived to place the dressing over the catheter, they told me Wil had walked in and out of the apartment and dialysis clinic. I worried that the pressure from all the walking would deteriorate his wound even further. Before leaving I reminded them to offer medication to keep any pain at bay.

That night around ten p.m., Ellen called me because Wil was having a lot of pain and she reported he was angry with her for attempting to medicate him. He was quite agitated and reaching for things above him, talking to others not visible in the room. This was scaring her, and she requested I make a visit. When I arrived, Wil was still a bit restless. I spoke quietly to him, asking if he was in any pain. He confirmed he was, and I offered to give him some medicine to relieve it. He easily agreed and upon hearing this Ellen quickly left the room to retrieve the pain medication.

While she was gone, I asked Wil if he was feeling anxious or uneasy.

I asked the question I had asked hundreds of patients. "Are you feeling like you need to do something and you're not sure what it is?" He gave the same affirmative answer I usually received from patients who were aware they were preparing for something—a trip of sorts.

"Yes. That's it," he responded.

"It's normal to feel that way at this stage. Can I give you a little Ativan to help you relax? It may help to relieve this restless feeling too."

"Of course. I trust you know what to do," he said with some effort.

Ellen returned with the medicine and handed it to me.

"Thank you. Would you mind bringing in two spoons and the Ativan tabs?"

"Not at all." And she was gone. Like her mother she was happiest when busy with a task.

"I have the pain medicine for you. Here's your water to take it with. Okay?" I asked, reaching for the cup sitting on the bedside table.

Wil took the pill in one hand and the water in the other. I placed the straw in his mouth.

"Go easy, a little at a time." He hesitated before he swallowed. I knew small volumes, at this stage, could produce coughing fits. He took a tiny sip and then another.

"Oh, that is good. Nice and cold."

"Would you like more?" I asked.

"No, that was enough."

Ellen had returned with two spoons and the bottle of Ativan I had requested. I knew Wil was beginning to have trouble swallowing pills and thought it wouldn't hurt to start teaching them the options for administering medications in oral syringes. I gave some instruction to her as I placed the small tab on one spoon, the other spoon over it, and pressed to crush it.

"Then draw up about a quarter to a third of a dropper of water and place it on top of the powder. Stir it like this with the tip of the syringe and when it has all dissolved, pull back on the plunger of the syringe until all the liquid is inside."

"Oh, great. What a good idea," she said.

"Yes. It makes it easy to administer meds like this when patients can no longer swallow them whole. Then lace it between his gums and cheek on either side."

"Got it," she said.

I looked at my friend, who was intently watching the teaching moment.

"I have a great team, don't I?" he asked, finding the positive in any situation, as usual.

In unison, we responded, "Yes!" We laughed at the synchronicity of it.

"I know you're tired, so we don't want to keep you up. Let me just give you this Ativan." Wil easily swallowed the small dropper of medicine. "If it is okay, I will sit here while you rest to be sure the medicines are keeping you comfortable."

"Oh, fine, if it's not putting you out," he was able to say.

"Not at all. I would be glad to." I winked at Ellen who bent down to kiss her dad.

"Good night. I will see you in the morning, Papa."

"Good night," he said and smiled at her.

The house was quiet within fifteen minutes. Wil's furrowed brow and restlessness were no longer evident. I sat in his recliner at the bedside and thankfully saw no signs of discomfort or restlessness for the remainder of the night. He slept for eight hours and so did the tired caregivers.

In the morning I left written instructions for Ellen regarding what to administer and how frequently, if the symptoms were to appear again. I talked to Doris about the changes in Wil and reminded her to call me if she had any questions or concerns in the coming days. When I suggested he might be getting closer to his final days she made it clear to me she didn't want to discuss it. I respectfully let it go. I had learned you have to allow people to open up to this discussion on their own timeline.

Tim arrived early to help with his dad's care. Ellen and Tim stayed at the bedside during the morning while Wil slept; when he woke, he asked what was going on.

"We think you might be dying," Tim responded honestly.

"I think you might be right," Wil agreed.

The next morning, he was more lucid and more like his old self. Ellen and Tim had alerted the immediate family about the "close call" so they could visit one more time if they wanted to. They had not made Wil aware of these phone calls, but in the intuitive fashion I had witnessed in many patients, he somehow knew. In fact, when his granddaughter Molly arrived for a visit, as she entered the apartment he looked up from his lunch and said, "You thought I'd be dead when you got here, didn't you!" with a twinkle in his eye and a chuckle. The family gasped and then burst out laughing.

Over the next two weeks I continued my visits and enjoyed our time together during his treatments. Life went on. Ellen returned to her home and checked in several times a day by phone. Tim continued his routine of visiting three to four times a week and sometimes stayed to enjoy a meal with them.

Then one afternoon I received a call from Tim saying his dad had fallen outside in the driveway of the dialysis center and had been taken to the local hospital by ambulance. He said Wil had only sustained bruises and a few scrapes. Tim wondered if I could possibly meet them at the hospital to transport his parents back home. I told him I could be on my way in about an hour, as I was finishing up a patient consult in a nearby hospital. He thanked me and said he appreciated my quick response and ability to get them settled back at home after leaving the hospital.

When I arrived, Wil had been moved to the medical office area of the hospital. His wounds had been cleaned and covered. He had a bump on his head, and he was having some pain in his leg. The nurse assured me they saw no need for an MRI of the brain, as Wil had sustained only a small contusion. His leg was X-rayed and no fractures were noted. The doctor recommended over-the-counter acetaminophen for the pain or using the tramadol he already had at home. Once the report had been given, Tim was able to head back to work and told his parents he would see them later, thanking me again for being on call for them.

The nurse reviewed the dressing change frequency with us, then she told Wil he could go back home but encouraged him to call if any major changes occurred like nausea, vomiting, or a severe headache.

I wheeled him to the exit and helped him into my car. Doris had driven their car over so we met in the parking lot of their apartment. I asked Doris to stay with him while I went into the apartment to retrieve the transport chair. My heart went out to Doris as I wheeled the chair out. I knew she was feeling terrible about not taking my or Ellen's advice about using it to avoid a fall. I hugged her once I reached the car.

"These things happen. It is not your fault," I said, hoping to dilute her guilt. "Let's get him in the chair and get you both inside. You must be starving."

"What shall I do?" she asked.

"If you can hold the handles of the chair it would be a great help. I've locked the wheels, but sometimes the chair still moves a bit." She took her position holding the handles tightly. She looked so frail and tiny to me.

"Ready?" I said to my friend who was sitting sideways on the car seat, with his feet outside the car on the pavement.

"If you hold on to this handle on the car door and pull yourself forward, I will hold you under your arm and lift you up at the same time. Okay?"

"Okay," he said reaching for the door handle.

"One, two, three. Up we go."

He stood up slowly and needed my support to stand.

"Okay, now I am going to have you hold on to the car here and I will hold you again while you take tiny steps to turn this way, so you can sit there." I pointed to the seat to his right. He took the tiny sideways steps in slow motion, with a grimace, and when he was aligned with the seat of the transport chair I spoke again.

"This time I want you to put both hands on the armrests and then I will help to lower you slowly. Here we go."

He searched with his hands until he found the armrests and bent forward as he began to sit. I held him under his arms to slow him down. He moaned as we lowered him to the seat.

"I'm sorry if it hurts to move. Let me get the footrests under your feet." He was too weak to lift his feet, so I eased them into place.

"Great teamwork!" I said to the two of them once he was settled.

Then we made our way to the upper entry door, so there were no stairs to contend with. Wil and Doris were both hungry and exhausted from the emotional events of the day.

"I'm going to call down to the kitchen to ask for our dinner to be served here tonight," Doris announced, once we were inside the apartment.

"Good idea. I'll get Wil set up at the table."

"I am starving!" he said, once seated.

"I'm not surprised. The small snacks you had at the hospital were hardly a lunch. I bet dinner will be here soon enough." I encouraged Wil to take the tramadol for his pain before eating his meal and he agreed.

Doris set to work getting the dishes, silverware, and drinks on the table.

"Would you like to join us?" she asked.

"Oh no. Thank you, though. I'll be happy to see the two of you enjoy a nice hot meal." I smiled at them, thinking I would like to get him into bed before leaving, but didn't mention it; one thing at a time.

A knock at the door came soon and the warm meals with their wonderful aroma were a welcome sight for my two hungry, tired, and emotionally drained friends. They ate quietly with a few comments about how delicious it was, offering me food again which I graciously declined.

Once Wil finished, I took the opportunity, though it was only five thirty, to ask if I could help him to bed. He easily agreed saying he was ready for a good night's sleep. Doris thanked me, saying she was tired too and appreciated having the help. Wil was asleep within minutes of lying down.

I sat with Doris in the living room and told her to be sure to offer the tramadol pain medicine every four to six hours in order to keep Wil comfortable. I asked her to call me day or night with any concerns and suggested I visit the next day to be sure his pain was under control and assess his scrapes. She said she would appreciate such a visit. I hugged her and wished her a good night's sleep, then let myself out.

In the coming days, Wil's pain increased. Doris told me she was having difficulty knowing when to medicate him because he struggled to articulate his needs and would not ask for medication. Like many caregivers, she said she was reluctant to give him the pain medications, worried it might be too much, so if he didn't ask, she didn't offer. This is a sad and common scenario that has evolved with the overprescribing of opioids.

I decided to talk to Wil about attaining comfort even if it meant his sleeping more. We had returned from another treatment and Wil was tired and clearly in pain again. I knew this was going to be a difficult discussion for Doris—understandably so.

"Can I ask you a question about how you want us to treat your pain?" I said as I placed the protective dressing over his catheter. Doris was sitting across from him in her chair as I spoke.

"Of course, please share some of your …" He stumbled to find the word. "Oh, I can't think of the word," he said, frustrated.

"Insight?" Doris suggested.

"Yes, that's it. Insight," he agreed.

"I want to be sure I am honoring your wishes. You are having more pain since your fall and you don't ask for pain medicine. This makes it hard for Doris to know when to give it to you. I would like to schedule it three times a day, to try to keep the pain from getting out of control. I could add it to your med planner to make it easier on both of you."

"Is that too much?" Doris asked.

"I don't want this pain," he told her.

"A long time ago we talked about how sometimes in order to totally relieve pain, it can mean the person is sleeping more. What do you think about this now?" I asked Wil, hoping he would still choose comfort.

"I don't want to feel the pain like I have been. I would rather sleep," he articulated clearly.

"You haven't been up and walking as much," Doris told him. "You have to keep moving to stay strong. I don't want you to sleep all day, honey, and if you get drowsy from the medicine, I'm afraid you'll fall."

I listened, knowing this was a legitimate concern, but let them attempt to work through it on their own.

"Well, I don't want to be in pain either." He was clear and to the point again.

"Okay, honey, no pain. I understand."

"Having the tramadol three times a day should help relieve your pain, but not be overly sedating. I'm bringing this question up now while we can discuss it. Otherwise, if you were to be in a severe pain crisis and we had not discussed it, we wouldn't know if we were respecting your choices. Now we know you would choose comfort, even if it means sleeping more." I reviewed his response to be sure I had understood and that Doris had too.

"Your fentanyl patch offers a low dose of pain relief around the clock, but you still need medication for the pain if it breaks through. Does this make sense?"

Wil and Doris were quiet for a minute, pondering the tough discussion, clearly in different camps. I could understand Doris not wanting to consider her husband only sleeping and possibly no longer speaking to her. I could also understand my friend not wanting to endure daily pain. I waited for confirmation.

"Honey? What are you thinking?" he inquired in his gentle and thoughtful way.

"I don't want you to have pain either, but I don't like to think about you lying there and not being able to talk to us."

He nodded. "I understand. I would like to try this."

"Let's hope the fentanyl patch along with the regular doses of tramadol will be enough to keep you comfortable," I said, hoping to offer her realistic encouragement about the need for scheduling the tramadol. I understood she was doing the best she could in letting go of her husband, in tiny steps—clearly unwelcome tiny steps.

"I hope so," she said, sighing.

At my next visit, on Thursday, Ellen had arrived to help out and told me there had been another family meeting to discuss whether Wil felt he was nearing the end of his life. Before answering, Wil asked his children and wife, one by one, if they would be okay financially. They each said they would be all right. Then he asked, "Is my work done?" They replied that it was. Finally, he asked, "How does it happen? Is there a pill I will take?" They explained to Wil that when he felt ready, he should tell them, and dialysis would be stopped, and he would likely only live for a few days to two weeks afterward.

Hearing this, Wil said, "I feel used up and am at the end of the road." So together they discussed stopping the treatments shortly after his birthday, which they would celebrate on Thanksgiving. This would give them another chance to gather as a family and cherish the final moments with the man who had been the patriarch, spiritual leader, great lifelong teacher, and counselor for the family.

That afternoon, Ellen was present during a physical therapy visit and told the therapist the family had talked to Wil about whether he felt he was getting closer to being ready to die. The therapist was initially shocked to hear this, but said, knowing Wil, he was not surprised he had talked so openly about dying. "How long do you think it will be until you die?" the therapist asked Wil directly.

"Two weeks," Wil responded, with confidence.

I will never forget being with Wil, Doris, Tim, and Ellen, two days later on Saturday. The CD with Wil's favorite songs was playing and they were singing along and laughing together. Wil was moving his foot to the tune of the music and holding Doris's hand. I loved the joyful music too, so I joined in the fun.

After a few songs, Ellen took me aside to tell me, with some excitement, her dad had been having some amazing conversations with them about what he was seeing and learning on his *journey*, as he called it. I was so happy they were having these conversations and thankful Wil was sharing his experiences. Some patients share little about what they are seeing and planning. Hearing this directly from him, especially with his advanced dementia, was nothing short of amazing. I was also grateful they were being prepared for his death by him and not by me. This would be more powerful and make accepting the inevitable easier if they knew it was his plan.

Visits from his old neighbor, his niece, granddaughter, and his only brother were helping him share his good memories and allowing for mutual goodbyes. I began to notice a bit more acceptance by the two most important women in his life. They were enjoying every moment, shared meal, laughter, and conversation with him, in a bittersweet way.

The next Tuesday, when I arrived to sit with him at his first treatment of the week, the clinic nurse warned me he had been anxious, tugging at his catheter and asking to go home. I told her the family was planning to stop the treatments in about three weeks, due to his frequent requests. She said the staff had noticed he was becoming more and more restless during treatments and scratching at the catheter regularly, complaining of it itching. They understood he was coming to the end of the road with regard to the burden outweighing the benefit of his treatments. She said they would miss seeing him.

As I settled into a chair next to him, he asked why he had to continue having the treatments, he had forgotten the family discussion. I told him he had given his family a gift of two and a half years by agreeing to do the treatments—treatments he never wanted to start in the first place. An unselfish gift for sure. He said he didn't regret the decision, then tried to articulate how much he disliked having to sit for so many hours, three times each week. I listened to the long explanation; Wil struggled to find the words, at times. My friend who had been an articulate man of deep thought all of his life, now struggled to piece a sentence together. I sat patiently, listening, and trying to imagine how frustrating it must be for him, wondering if he remembered his old mind.

Once he was done putting as many words together as he was able, in his attempt to express his thoughts, I told him I understood. I sat and waited for him to speak again, and we began our usual conversation to pass the time. We both enjoyed reminiscing about our friendship and common friends. He liked these conversations, and they seemed to jog his long-term memory. It helped to distract him and reduce his stress and anxiety, and before we knew it, his treatment was done. I assisted him into his transport chair and we headed out the door to my car.

The next time I saw him was for his second treatment of the week, and it turned out to be the last. I met his son Tim at the apartment. He had arrived at five a.m. to get his father dressed and out the door on time. I demonstrated how to transfer Wil into the car from the transport chair and asked Tim to follow us to the clinic and try transferring Wil on his own. Wil moaned with the transfer; the leg injury he had sustained in the fall was causing pain when he put weight on it.

On our ride I said, "I'll ask the nurse at the clinic to give you some Tylenol for the leg pain."

Wil asked, "What is this visit we are going to?"

"It's your dialysis treatment."

"I'm at the end of this. And that's okay." Wil announced.

"Are you tired of them, Wil?"

"Yes."

"Are you ready to be done?" I asked, meaning done with life.

In his usual intuitive fashion, he knew what I meant and responded, "I am. Death is not a threat, it's a welcome reception."

Wow! Wil's ability to articulate his thoughts, for brief periods, at this stage of his dementia was astounding. Once we arrived at the clinic, Tim transferred his dad out of my car and into the transport chair; Wil's moans were making it clear that it was time to stop.

"This is really painful for him, Tim," I said.

"I know, I think this is the last treatment." Tim pushed the chair and we walked behind Wil across the parking lot.

"He wants to be done," I said. "He just told me that death is not a threat, it's a welcome reception."

"He said that?"

"He did. He has been waiting for all of you to be ready."

"I'll talk to my mom and Ellen this morning."

Tim stopped pushing the chair and bent down next to his father, placing his hand on Wil's. "This is the last treatment, Dad."

"Good." Wil smiled at his son and patted his hand in a comforting way, knowing this was going to be harder on Tim than it was on him.

"I'll see you later, Dad," Tim said as he stepped aside to let me push the chair.

I breathed a huge sigh of relief as we crossed the threshold into the clinic—still wanting to just turn around and go home. I told the nurse Wil was experiencing some leg pain and requested some Tylenol. She returned quickly with the pills and some water before beginning his treatment.

After he was settled and his treatment had begun I asked, "Is there anything you're worried about or afraid of?"

"Is there a pill or something I can take to make things go along quickly?"

"No. I remember you had asked for that option and decided to do dialysis for a time to allow your family to prepare to say goodbye to you. You have gone on for two and a half years."

"Ahh," he said.

"Are you feeling ready to die Wil?" I asked, wondering if he still remembered the conversation during our car ride over.

"Oh, yes. Are there things I need to help them with?"

"No, Wil, they understand. You've been preparing them. You've been doing lots of work, getting ready to die. You've been reaching out and talking to loved ones who have died. You've told us about both your mom and dad being with you."

"My mom is not quite ready for me yet; my dad is there."

"Are you getting your questions answered? They're there to guide you, Wil."

"I think so. Is there a drink I can have to move this along to its end place?"

"No, there isn't a drink. The work you are doing is moving you along."

"Is there anything else I need to be doing?"

"You're doing everything just beautifully, Wil. Thank you for allowing me to accompany you and to help you and your family."

"Oh, I think I say thank you for the things …" He paused, trying to hold on to his train of thought, I imagined like trying to reel in a fighting fish. "… the part you gave," he concluded.

"You're welcome, my friend," I said, and then stood to give him a kiss on the forehead.

Wil slept while the machine cleaned his blood for the last time. I sat looking at him and thinking about the changes in his face, his body, and most of all, his mind. Changes brought on by diseases that had been slowly stealing away his joy, his personality, his sharp mind, his physical strength, and his ability to enjoy reading, writing, and deep conversations—all the things he had so loved. From the moment we met I knew he was a gifted person, sent to make the world a better place, and he had. In his profound abilities he had not lost this principal aspect of himself—his innate wisdom still there through it all.

When he woke, he surprised me again when he quite eloquently shared this conversation with me. Before we started, I asked Wil if I could record our discussion so we could share it with his family, and he agreed.

I asked him, "What do you want your family to know?"

This is what Wil said: "A situation where they're letting it go downhill because it's time. And not have to rush with medical treatments to fulfill something that is a dead-end anyway and we know it. It's okay, because, let it go. Let it be where it is."

"You feel ready to go?" I asked, to clarify.

"I feel ready, there's no question."

"You've had an amazing life. You've affected many people, including me." I paused to take a deep breath to hold the emotion back so I could continue to speak.

"And you will be so missed. But never forgotten." I choked on my emotions.

"Well, it went pretty well. Not too many regrets." He thought it over and smiled—ever the optimist.

"Wow, how about that! That's a life well lived."

"Not all the way, but most of the way. Not many regrets."

"Is there anything you want to do or say now? Any other things left unsaid?"

Wil sat thinking and I wondered if we had lost the precious window of clarity. After about a minute, I asked, "How about the bowl of ice cream we talked about earlier?"

We both laughed, and he said, "Oh ho!"

"What's your favorite flavor?" I asked, knowing the answer but hoping to keep the conversation going.

"Coffee, I think."

"There is a fresh box of coffee ice cream in your freezer. I just happen to know it. Ellen bought a new one so you could have a nice dish of ice cream."

"Mmm."

"They know how you love ice cream." Then, seeing he was drifting away, I closed the conversation.

"Thank you for talking. I think it will help your family to hear this message."

"I feel that it's a pretty good family. They have really done important things and they have given me a lot."

I was thankful to have had the conversation and amazed at his ability to express his desires.

Ellen was arriving in the early afternoon, so I suggested we could play the message after lunch. He liked the idea. I knew Wil and Doris napped after lunch, so as we finished eating, I opened the conversation and then played Wil's message for Doris and Ellen while we were still at the table. After hearing it they knew what he was asking them to do. They understood he was telling them it was time to stop his treatments and allow him to die; he didn't want to wait until Thanksgiving and his birthday to arrive. Tim had already forewarned them.

We discussed having hospice services again and because he was a retired minister, they said their strong connection to the local church was more comfortable for them than meeting an unknown hospice chaplain. Likewise, funeral plans were all in place and the advance directives had been completed more than two years prior. Instead of signing up for hospice services they would increase my hours and utilize my hospice nurse experience. Doris again expressed relief, saying all the new faces coming into the home would have been overwhelming for her.

I made a call to Wil's primary doctor's office to inform them treatments were stopping. It was Thursday afternoon, and I offered to start visiting daily in order to assess him, ensure his comfort, and support them. They wholeheartedly agreed with the plan, stating they would appreciate the daily support.

I explained they might notice Wil sleeping more, eating less, and having end-of-life conversations with others they would not be able to see. I alerted them to watch for a *looking-through-you-not-at-you* effect to his eyes, a good sign he was preparing to make his way. I reminded them these were all normal end-of-life behaviors and observing and allowing him to do this necessary work was the best support they could offer him.

"We can't help with this part. He must do it himself and in his own time," I explained.

When I visited the next day, I was told he had eaten a light breakfast in bed since he was too weak to get up and had refused lunch. Doris was concerned about his minimal interest in food, so I tried to comfort her. I explained it was quite common to be less interested in food and it was best to allow him to eat or drink what appealed to him.

Ellen reported he had been up quite a bit throughout the night. She observed his busy hands and arms moving above his chest, as we had discussed on the previous day. She had also noticed he seemed to be having a quiet conversation and she tried to ask him about it, but he didn't respond and continued on. She said she found all of this quite fascinating. I was glad she could take in the instinctual power of the dying process at work.

I asked Doris and Ellen if they would give me a few minutes to privately assess him, and then we could talk again. They agreed and stayed in the kitchen. I found my friend resting peacefully in his bed, his favorite CD playing softly in the background. I stopped to stare at him as he slept, thinking our precious friendship was coming to an end and he would soon stop speaking to me—to all of us.

I took in a deep breath of gratitude for having been part of his life and for our close friendship. He had confided in me and trusted me during some challenging times in his career life and, in those moments, I questioned my worthiness for such a position. At the same time, because I trusted his great wisdom, I understood I had some ability to support him beyond my own understanding.

During one of these times, and there were only a few, I said I felt unworthy because I saw him as the teacher. He laughed and responded he had learned so much from me. I was shocked to learn this. He went on to tell me what he had learned. Ultimately, he was teaching me again about how we affect others and often are unaware.

I sat on the edge of the bed and counted his respirations: twelve, beginning to slow, as would be expected at this stage of the dying process. I held his wrist and with my first two fingers gently pressed until I felt his radial pulse. I counted for fifteen seconds—25 x 4 = 100. Going up slightly, also as expected. I slid my hand into his palm; it was warm, not clammy or cold. His face was flushed. I gently touch his forehead—clammy. I was experiencing an inner struggle of hospice nurse knowing her patient was nearing death, and friend not wanting to part with her dear friend and mentor. I looked at him again, thinking it was quite amazing that, somehow, I was actually there with him, on the major precipice of his life, when he was so close to crossing over. I closed my eyes, silently thanking him for all he had shared with me, I knew he could hear me. I had shared the life-changing lessons he taught me with others in need; thereby, together, we sent great ripples across the pond.

While Wil slept, I thought about what I wanted to say to him in thanks for so many great years of friendship. I believe, in this phase of the dying process, patients are able to communicate in ways we are unaware of, mostly because we ignore those abilities. Patients often verbalized awareness of discussions that had not been shared with them, predicted unexpected visitors, and answered unspoken questions.

After about five minutes, Wil stirred. I was still holding his hand when he opened his eyes.

"Hello, Ellie," he said, remembering my name.

"How are you, my friend?" I gently squeezed his hand.

"I'm doing okay."

"Are you in any pain?"

"No pain at the moment."

"Are you worried about anything or anyone?"

"No. I am feeling ready to go, and at peace about it."

I was amazed by his verbal ability.

"I know the kids will take great care of her." Wil nodded in the direction of the kitchen where Doris could be heard talking to Ellen.

"I'm so glad. Do you think they are ready?"

"I don't know. What do you think?" Wil asked.

"I think Doris will never be ready to say goodbye to you. The kids are here to help her, and I will do my best. I can tell you they have all told me they want you to be out of pain and find peace when you are ready."

"Oh, good," he said.

"We planned to get you washed up, and to change your clothes this morning. I would like to give you medication before we reposition you, okay?"

"Sure. I trust you know what's best."

I was witnessing a small miracle. His ability, with his moderate dementia, to be so present in his conversations was teaching me about connecting deeply to innate spiritual power.

"I'll get the medicine and be right back," I said.

I went to the kitchen and found Doris and Ellen sitting in silence and sipping tea at the kitchen table. I explained that we should medicate him before we washed him and changed his clothing. Ellen retrieved the liquid oxycodone from the refrigerator and drew up the small 10 milligram dose into the oral syringe.

"Shall I give it?" she asked.

"Sure. Thank you. I'll be right in." I wanted to speak with her mom privately to see how she was digesting all of the changes in Wil. I sat next to her at the table.

"How are you doing today?"

"I'm okay. But I don't understand why it's changing so fast. Yesterday, he went out for his treatment, then he slept most of the afternoon. He barely ate breakfast this morning and didn't want any lunch."

"I know this is hard for you, Doris. I'm sorry. You're all doing a fantastic job of caring for him. Were you able to sleep last night?" I asked, knowing Ellen had been up frequently with her dad.

"I did sleep well. I was so exhausted."

"Well, I'm glad you were able to get in a good night's sleep. This constant care is pretty exhausting emotionally and physically, isn't it?"

"Yes. Thank God for the kids. I couldn't do it without them."

"They are great," I agreed. "He may only want sips of water from here on out. This is okay," I continued, hoping to decrease her anxiety around his choice to eat little to nothing.

"Really?"

I took her hand. "This is the hardest part for so many caregivers. Please don't think he is starving. He is choosing to have only liquids now. He's done this, many times before, when he guided the vision quests in Death Valley, remember?"

"Oh yes. You're right. I think he once went for three days without eating."

"All those years ago, he was preparing for this time."

She was pensive, then replied, "Yes, I suppose he was."

"Do you have any questions for me?"

"No, not really."

"Well thanks for talking with me. I'm going to check back in with them. Ellen and I are going to wash him once the medicine has had time to work."

"Okay. I'm going to do the dishes," she said, and was up in a flash. Busy was her middle name! She was one of the most disciplined and organized people I had ever met—never wasting a moment. When I returned to the bedroom, Ellen was sitting on the right side of the bed in a chair. I returned to my seat on the left side of the bed next to Wil. As I sat down, he looked up, smiled, and then held out his hand, asking for mine.

Oh, help me to keep my emotions in check, I thought, as I sat holding hands with my dear friend, who clearly had something to say.

"Ellie how are *you* doing?" he asked. It was all I could do to stop my jaw from dropping. I glanced at Ellen, grinned, then looked back at him.

"Oh, only you would be asking how *I'm* doing at such a time!" I laughed.

He carefully articulated this response. "No, I mean it. This is not easy for you." He paused for a minute, and we remained quiet, allowing the word search to take its course.

"I appreciate your great care of me and my family ... and I want you here, but hope it is not too much for you," he said, with the full compassion of the man I had known for years.

"Well, I want to tell you it is my utmost privilege to be here for you and your family. I thank you all for allowing me in."

Again, he slowly shared his thoughts, searching for a word or two.

"I had hoped you could be here for me at the end of my life. I'm so glad it worked out."

My deep breath in was unsuccessful; a few tears escaped my efforts to hold them back. I continued to stare at my friend, who seemed to be defying his body and brain. I found my courage and then spoke again.

"Years ago, when you told me about your wish for me to be with you when you were dying, I hoped for it too. I wondered if it would actually be able to happen, not knowing where I might be working years down the road, or where you might be living. I never imagined I would be working for myself and offering private duty services. It is quite amazing and wonderful how it all worked out."

Tears rolled down Ellen's cheeks as Wil and I carried on.

"I want to thank you for all the wisdom and guidance you offered me over the years, Wil. I've learned so much from you, and I will always consider it a gift to have been called your friend."

It was all I could say without totally losing my composure. I leaned down and he wrapped his arms around my neck to hug me. I knew this was a conversation and moment I would treasure and carry with me. I would recount it on many days in the future when I missed his great presence, joy, and friendship.

"That was beautiful!" Ellen chimed in. "I hope it was okay I stayed to listen."

"Of course," Wil and I responded in unison and then laughed at our still strongly connected thoughts.

The laughter was exactly what we needed to move us forward.

"Shall we get you washed up and into a clean T-shirt?" I asked him, hoping for an affirmative response, though knowing it could cause some pain when we repositioned him.

"Sure."

"We'll reposition you slowly to keep the discomfort to a minimum."

Ellen gathered a washbasin, some washcloths, and towels. The three of us worked together to give him a sponge bath and place his clean clothes on his fragile frame. Even with our efforts to use the draw sheet under him and roll him slowly, he still had some discomfort. I knew we might be approaching the time when comfort and sedation would win out over alertness. I planned to follow his choice if we needed to maintain his comfort and accept the sedating side effect of a larger dose of pain medication.

Being not only his nurse but a close friend, I kept him covered from the waist down with the sheet as we worked on washing his upper body, and he washed privately. Discretely, with the sheet still in place, I was able to assist him with getting his underclothing back on. Ellen helped him into a clean T-shirt and then we were done; he was exhausted.

"I think we will let you sleep. How does that sound?" I asked once we had put away the washbasin and towels.

"I'm pretty tired after all the movement," he admitted.

"Would you like anything to eat or drink before you nap, Papa?" Ellen asked.

"Yes, I would love some ice-cold water." You could hear the thirst in his voice.

Ellen went out and, no sooner had she left, Doris came in.

"Well, you look fresh," she said, bending down to kiss him.

"Yes, we three worked together and now I'm tired and going to have a nap," Wil proclaimed clearly.

"Aren't you hungry? You didn't have lunch," Doris said.

"Here you go, Papa." Ellen had returned with a tall, covered cup of ice water.

"Thank you. This is all I want," he said, taking a long, slow drink. "Ahh, tastes so good." And then he took another long sip. "Would you put this on the bedside table, honey, please?" he asked Doris, who placed it next to the bed.

"Okay, well, maybe you'll be hungry when you wake," she said, not losing hope for her cause to feed him again—a loving gesture.

"We'll see," Wil responded. I imagined, knowing all too well, it would not be the case.

"I'm going to say goodbye," I said to them.

"Will I see you tomorrow?" Wil asked with a smile.

"You bet. I'll be coming every day if it's still okay."

"I would appreciate it if you could. Thank you, Ellie," my friend said, using my name again.

"You're welcome. I hope you can have a nice deep sleep." I took his hand and gently squeezed it, then leaned down and kissed his forehead. "Sweet dreams."

On my drive home I was thinking about our conversation and how he had been so lucid, his old self, caring for others, knowing details. Even in his final days, with the interference of dementia on his thoughts, my dear friend was still somehow able to show me the extraordinary person we had all come to know, even using my name again, which he hadn't been able to do for many months.

On Saturday, Wil rested, while Doris, Tim, and Ellen took turns sitting with him. During my visit I medicated him and then changed the dressing covering the wound on his foot. Tim helped me with washing Wil and getting him repositioned and comfortable using a small pillow between his ankles to keep the pressure off.

I checked in with Ellen via text messages later in the day and again before going to bed. Wil had been sleeping off and on throughout the afternoon and evening. She reported he seemed a little restless. I called her so we could have an actual phone conversation. I'm a dinosaur and still prefer talking on the phone or in person over text messaging.

I encouraged her to crush an Ativan tab and lace it (slowly moving forward between the cheek and gums) into his cheek if he was too tired to swallow the tab whole. I reminded her it could be given again in four to six hours, if needed. I also offered to come and stay with Wil so she could get some rest. She thanked me, but said she was up to it and wanted to have the precious time with her dad. She said she could see some of the beautiful and amazing details that came with dying, and she appreciated the privilege of being there to witness them.

Ellen called me early the next morning. Her dad seemed to be having more pain and she was afraid to move him. I offered to head right over and she quickly accepted. I could hear the exhaustion and concern in her voice. I packed up my things, brushed my teeth, and was out the door in five minutes.

Once I had arrived, I immediately saw the anxiety on both women's faces. I understood it was difficult and unsettling to see someone you love in pain. I hugged them both and then headed straight to the bedroom in order to assess my friend.

I could see his grimace and furrowed brow, both signs of pain. I set my nursing bag on the chair and took off my coat and placed it over the back of the chair. I rubbed sanitizer into my hands and then continued to rub them together to make sure they were warm as I approached the bed. I took my usual position sitting on the bed next to him. I took his hand; he did not open his eyes. I leaned down toward him.

"Are you in a lot of pain, Wil?" I whispered in his ear.

Sadly, my friend nodded yes. My heart sank.

"I'm so sorry. We're going to get you some medicine right now. If we have to trade being alert for sleeping and being out of pain, is this still what you want?"

"Yes," he whispered.

I wanted to honor his previous request for no pain, even at the risk of sedation, and I was relieved to have that confirmed—although, had he not answered I would have done it anyway, knowing that was his wish. I returned to the kitchen to review the overnight administration of oxycodone from the paper tracking sheet we had made. It looked like the 10 milligram dose was no longer working; it was time to increase the breakthrough dose. I medicated him and sat at his bedside praying it would work fast to give him some comfort. Doris and Ellen came in and out of the room, anxiously checking in as I waited to reassess. He appeared to relax within about fifteen minutes—it seemed like forever as we waited. Once his brow was relaxed, with no sign of clenched fists or grimacing, I went out to the living room to report he was resting comfortably.

"I think it's working now. He seems more comfortable. But I think we should start medicating him at regular intervals and at 15 milligram doses now, in order to keep the pain at bay. It's so hard to get pain under control when it reaches higher levels."

"That makes sense," Ellen agreed.

"But we don't want to give him too much either," Doris protested.

"At this point, we can't give him too much if we follow the doctor's order. Keeping him comfortable and peaceful is what he indicated was his desire, even if it means sedation, so we are honoring his wishes, as we had promised."

"I guess so," she said.

"We'll need to medicate him every four to six hours, so the pain doesn't get out of control. If he seems comfortable, we can push the intervals out slightly. Does that make sense?"

"Yes. Don't you think so, Mom?" Ellen asked.

Doris nodded, still struggling to accept the loss of his alertness … forever.

"Even though he is not talking much, he can still hear us. Is there anything you want to say that you haven't said in recent days?"

"No. I can't get over how fast this has happened," Doris said, shaking her head.

"Mom, I know this hard, but Papa told us he was tired and ready to go. Remember last week when he said to us, "Ta-ta, I have to be going," with a chuckle? Wasn't it amazing how he kept his great humor?" Ellen said, trying to lift her mom's spirits.

Doris laughed. "Yes. He was enjoying his music and laughing last week; it was so wonderful." She let out a deep sigh.

I couldn't imagine the depth of this moment for her breaking heart and the unwelcome changes in her life that were waiting in the very near future.

"We have successfully managed his pain, and this was important, not only for him, but for all of you." I said. "I hope it will do your hearts good to see him resting comfortably."

Doris surrendered. "I don't want him to be in pain anymore either. How long will it take, Ellie?" She was ready to accept the loss, and I felt what had seemed the weight of a boulder lift off my shoulders. Thank you, I thought. Now help me find the words to comfort her.

"I can't say for sure," I said. "We've watched him having the necessary conversations with those on the other side. He's done his best to talk to and prepare all of you. He's done a lot of amazing work, hasn't he?" I hoped she could see the process more clearly now.

"Yes, he really has. What happens next?" she asked. Ellen watched her mother's acceptance unfold.

"He'll continue to sleep. We'll need to keep him comfortable using his pain medicine and offering mouth care, but we won't be moving him around too much anymore. We'll rotate the pillow under his back from side to side, so he doesn't get sore from resting in the same position for too long."

"Okay, we can do it. Right?" Doris looked to Ellen for confirmation.

"Yes, Mom. We can do it. And the rest of the family will help us if we ask them."

"I don't want a lot of company; it's too much for me now," she admitted.

"Okay, Mom. Some of them might want to say goodbye to him, though." A long silence fell, allowing time to consider the idea.

"I guess short visits are okay," Doris finally said.

"I think he's been waiting for all of you to be ready," I told

Doris. "As ready as you can ever be, of course. There's never a good time to say goodbye to someone we love." I waited, out of respect for the enormity of those words. Once she nodded, I went on.

"Sometimes seeing them in pain helps us to want them to find their peace and make their way."

She nodded. "That's true."

Knowing she had endured a long and difficult conversation, I tried to wrap up on a positive note.

"Thank you for allowing me to be here with you. Remember, even though he's not talking, he still hears you."

"You think he does hear us when he's sleeping?" she asked.

"Yes, I can promise you from years of doing this work, he will hear you. Sometimes patients who don't speak for days suddenly respond to a question or comment from their family. I think it's pretty amazing, no matter how many times I've witnessed it."

"Hmm. Okay. Well, I wanted to put in a load of wash, and if I get down there early there's no line for the washer."

"Good idea, Mom," Ellen responded, knowing keeping busy was the best medicine for her mother.

"I'm going to check on him and gather my things. Then I'll be heading home but call me if you need anything."

Doris went to the closet, retrieved her laundry basket, and headed out the door. I imagined she may have hoped to wash away the load of emotions she was feeling too.

I found Wil sleeping peacefully—no grimace, no furrowed brow, mouth wide open, slight phlegm beginning to accumulate in the back of his throat. I went to the refrigerator to retrieve the atropine drops so I could administer a dose in hopes of drying up the phlegm before it got out of control. I added a line on the medication tracking sheet and noted the time.

I gently pulled down his lower lip and placed two drops; he didn't respond. His respiration had slowed to ten per minute, due to the breaks in his breathing. I gently assessed his pulse at his wrist again. One hundred and thirty, indicating he was well on his way now that he was comfortable.

Ellen had been on the phone in the back bedroom talking with her brother, Tim, bringing him up to speed. When I entered the kitchen, she joined me and said he was planning to come by to spend a few hours sitting with his dad. She wanted to take a nap because she was exhausted from the little sleep of several nights in a row.

"I'm happy to come back tonight and sit with him so you can sleep," I offered.

"Really, Ellie?"

"I told you I would be here for you whenever you needed me. I'd be happy to sit with him and help you to catch up on some sleep."

"I could use some good sleep. Thank you so much."

"You're welcome. You're going to need the energy for the coming days."

"Do you think he is close?"

"I think he was waiting for all of you to be ready. We know he's been ready for a long time. Your mom is more accepting than ever before, and this will help him. All his hard work is done, and his physical body is preparing now. I don't think he'll converse anymore. Maybe a word here or there. When he's ready, he'll pick his time."

"It's so hard to imagine not having my dad to talk to and not seeing Mom and Dad together."

"I know. I'm sorry, Ellen." I hugged her for a minute while she wept.

Then I said, "You and Tim have done an amazing job of supporting your parents over these last few years. Please, don't ever forget this great gift you've given them. Your dad and mom both told me, on so many occasions, how much they appreciated having such wonderful, supportive children. I, of course, told them it was because of their amazing parenting," I said to lighten her heavy heart, and we both laughed. I removed my coat from the back of the kitchen chair.

"Okay, you need to rest, and I'll head home and be back later. What time would you like me to return? Anytime works for me," I said.

"I don't know. Eight or nine o'clock?"

"Why don't we talk later, and you can decide depending on how the day unfolds. All right?"

"Perfect, thanks again."

"As I keep telling you, it truly is my privilege to be here. Your dad is so special to me."

As I was about to open the door, Doris returned.

"Got it!" she said, snapping her fingers in the air. "The last washer."

"Oh, good, Mom. I asked Ellie to stay with Papa tonight so we could sleep."

"Is that okay with you?" Doris looked at me with concern.

"Of course. It would make me happy to know you two were getting some good sleep. Doris, I would be more than happy to stay with Wil."

"Oh, that's kind of you. I know it has been tiring for Ellen to be up so much with him at night," she said, looking toward Ellen.

"Yes. A good night's sleep is in order," I said with a smile. "He'll probably sleep most of the day. He'll need some mouth care, though, since he is sleeping with his mouth open now. Use the pink swabs we used this morning. I left half a dozen on the bedside table. You might also notice his eyes don't close all the way. This is common as well; he is so relaxed and working to find his peace." They both nodded.

"I'm going to rest in the recliner by his bed after lunch and I may nap after Tim arrives. In fact, Mom and I will probably both nap," Ellen concluded.

"Yes. I always nap after lunch," Doris said, raising her finger in the air.

"Thanks again for letting me help you," I said.

"Thank you. I'm so glad we have you and we can call you anytime with questions." This acceptance from Doris was good to hear at long last.

It was almost noon by the time I returned home. I packed an overnight bag with comfortable clothes, some toiletries, and a book. I decided I would bring my laptop, in case I wanted to read articles online.

Ellen and I texted during the late afternoon she updated me on his condition. *We continue to see pauses in his breathing, still sleeping with his mouth open. I gave him mouth care, he tolerated it well. I gave him atropine drops and liquid oxycodone again at four-hour marks as planned, no longer hearing any rumbling in his throat and he seems to be in no pain. Tim and I sat with him for a long time. Mom and I napped this afternoon.*

We planned for me to return around nine p.m. I texted when I pulled into the parking lot and Ellen met me at the locked exterior door. Before we entered the apartment, Ellen told me Tim had stayed for dinner and the three of them were able to have an open discussion about losing Wil and how it felt for each of them. I was so happy to hear this and knew my friend had heard it all with his heightened end-of-life senses—no doubt finding peace in it. Maybe exactly the peace he needed to go forward and not turn back again.

At precisely nine p.m., we entered the apartment quietly, gently closing and locking the door behind us, hoping not to wake Doris. I removed my coat and Ellen hung it in the kitchen closet for me. I picked up my nursing bag and overnight tote, then headed to the left side of the bed and set my things next to the rocker/recliner—the one Wil had always meditated in. This seemed like the perfect place to sit as I watched my dear friend, Wil, my *Gandhi,* my teacher as I had always called him, make his way out of this world. I wondered what he had left to teach me.

Ellen peeked in the door.

"Good night and sleep well. I'll wake you if anything changes," I whispered, knowing she worried about missing the final moments.

"Thank you," she whispered back, holding her hands in prayer position at her chest.

I heard the bedroom door close and went to sit at Wil's bedside, as I had done many times in recent days. I took in the moment, still surreal, even to this longtime hospice nurse. He's really going, I thought. I wondered who would greet him there, and who would be the next great teacher in my life when Wil was gone ... forever gone. *Just trust it*, came the answer—as if we were talking in our usual way. This was one of his common responses. *Just trust it.* I took a deep breath knowing he was right. Sitting with my hand holding his at his side, I began talking to him without speaking out loud.

How can I ever thank you for all you've taught me over these fifteen years of friendship? The fact that you even picked me to be called "dear friend" is still a bit of a wonder to me. To have someone as wise as you guiding me and teaching me as I explored and grew in my own spirituality, is one of the greatest gifts in my life. I am a much better person for knowing you. I promise I will never let go of what you've taught me, Wil. I will honor my purpose here, as much as I possibly can.

We sure did have some wonderful experiences caring for the dying, didn't we? I'll never forget how you calmed and comforted so many people with your gentle presence and openminded approach to prayer. You had an incredible ability to connect quickly and deeply with people of all faiths and those with none. I will treasure the many conversations we had about death and what we were witnessing. Conversations I couldn't have with any of my other colleagues. I am so thankful I had you to share in the excitement of witnessing some amazing things.

I know you're well on your way, and I am glad to see you resting peacefully with no signs of pain. I'll be right here with you all night ... (tears escaped now). *I love you, my friend. I will miss you so much, but I have a feeling your strong spirit will guide me from afar. I'll watch for the signs. It's time again, so I am going to medicate you and then let you rest.*

I placed two drops of atropine inside his lower lip, then laced a small amount of the liquid oxycodone in his cheek on one side, and then the other. I waited and watched while Wil swallowed hard and got it down without coughing. I repeated the process with the remaining half dose of liquid oxycodone in the dropper. He managed to swallow it down, again, without issue. Thankful for small favors, I quietly settled into the recliner with a blanket over my legs and my book, but I couldn't get into reading—my mind was too full.

I decided to take the opportunity to meditate in my teacher's meditation chair—another gift from my dear friend. I asked for guidance and wisdom in my life, going forward without my teacher to help me explore and discover my true spiritual self. He was the master of never telling me what to do, posing questions that made me think deeply. Eventually, I discovered my answers were right there all along. I possessed good intuition and had learned to listen from a young age. One of Wil's profound teaching gifts was helping me hone my intuition and push out the deceptive negative messages trying to derail my true path.

As I relaxed into my mediation, with Wil's rhythmic breathing and intermittent breaks in the background, two hours passed. At eleven p.m. I looked over at him still resting comfortably. I took my laptop out of my bag, which was lying next to the chair. I opened it and was about to go online to read an article when I suddenly felt compelled to open up a new Word document and start writing. This is what came out:

I'm starting to write my book as I sit at the bedside of my dying patient—something I have been trying to do for more than ten years, never able to find the right start, the right words. A pile of journals, with stories to inspire me, is always at my side with each attempt. Yet, I couldn't see the opening or the flow of the book. So back they would go into my bookcase, my feelings of disappointment returning. Now, at last, it has become clear to me how to weave the stories together.

I look at my patient resting comfortably in the bed and am grateful my years of pain and symptom management practice have allowed me to help him settle into a comfortable and peaceful place. He is well on his way in his dying process, as we call it in hospice.

I continued to write for two hours, as my dear friend and teacher did important work of his own. When I stopped writing, I knew my mentor had been at it again! Not telling me what to do but making me think, until I found the answer for myself. After ten years of attempting to start my book, it was finally underway —one last lesson from Wil, while he was still here on this Earthly plane.

He slept peacefully throughout the night. I backed off to every six hours on the medication intervals. Doris and Ellen were up around five a.m. and checked in. They were glad to see Wil resting peacefully, breathing calmly, with no sign of phlegm rumbling in his throat. They invited me to join them for oatmeal, the usual morning breakfast in their home. I accepted and was thankful to see them looking more rested and exhibiting greater peace and calm themselves.

I told Ellen Wil seemed to be getting close, but of course I could not predict the exact time. She immediately called Tim to inform him, and he said that he would be over soon to sit with his dad. During our breakfast, I asked if I could share the symbolic story Wil and I had been taught to use to help families let go of their loved ones.

"Wil shared this story countless times with families, as did I. I think it will help you with saying goodbye and letting him go," I said.

Doris and Ellen listened intently.

"Wil is on a ship leaving shore for a new destination. We are on the shore watching his ship slowly move away. Each time we reposition him now, touch his body frequently, or talk to him, we slow his ship down a little bit. This is okay because he gets underway again as soon as we're done interacting with him. But at some point, it will offer him more peace if we can let him keep on his way without interruption. He has worked hard to get this far and can see the horizon and what awaits him on the other side. Sometimes, we witness people reaching out, smiling, or saying someone's name during this phase."

"That's beautiful," Ellen said. Doris was taking it in with her own hopeful perspective, I imagined.

"I'm glad you think so, Ellen."

Then, knowing Doris didn't like talking about losing Wil, I said, "Thank you for a wonderful breakfast. Oatmeal is one of my favorites."

"You're welcome. We love it too," she responded, far off in thought.

I looked at Ellen. "I'll check in with you by text, so I don't disturb your time with him today. You could do the same or call with any questions at any time. I'll be visiting another patient around the corner at eleven and can stop by afterward," I suggested.

"That sounds good," Doris replied.

"Okay. I'll see you in a few hours." They both gave me a hug before I left.

On my drive home, I wondered how Wil would make his exit, who would be with him in the room when he died, and what time he would choose. I had learned from many patients they have control over these choices and the power of the spirit to wait for everything to be in order.

At ten thirty I got back in my car to head over to visit my patient who lived in the same area. As I drove down the familiar stretch of highway, I began thinking about how my friend was so mindful of how his decisions affected others. Whenever he requested a visit or a phone call with me, in order to hash something over with a trusted friend, he often said, "I hope I'm not putting you out."

It would not surprise me if Wil chose to die while I was in the area, because he wouldn't want me to have to come back later in the day. He wouldn't want to "put me out." I smiled and wondered again what he would choose. As I put my blinker on to take the exit for his town, my car phone rang. It was Ellen.

"Hi. Everything okay, Ellen?" I asked.

Her teary voice on the other end said, "He just died …"

"I'm so sorry. I'm only three minutes away."

"You are?" she said with some surprise.

"I'm turning off the exit."

"But how did you know?"

"I didn't. I was headed to see my other patient and then was going to stop by. Remember?"

"Oh, that's right. Do you need to go there first?"

"Oh no. I'll call her and tell her I need to make another visit and will see her later. I'll see you in two minutes."

"Thank you, Ellie. I can't believe he's gone."

"I know. I can't either," I said in disbelief, thinking the world had lost a great light. "Were you with him?" I was curious about what he had decided for his final moments.

"No. I had left the room in order to give Tim more time alone with him."

"What a blessing you were all in the home. How's your mom doing?"

"She's doing better than I thought she would in this moment."

"I'm so glad. I'm in the parking lot. I'll make my phone call and meet you at the door, Okay?"

"Thank you. I'll see you in a minute." And she was gone.

My other patient was understanding when I told her I had an unexpected visit I needed to make before coming to see her, and would she mind if I came in a few hours instead.

"Oh, not at all. Take your time," she responded.

As I walked up the path to Wil's home, it seemed surreal to me that this exceptional man could be gone from us. I couldn't imagine the depth of this loss for his family—his wisdom, humor, and deep love no longer present. Selfishly, I wondered again who would take his place as my mentor. I had such reverence for his teaching. Little did I know his lessons for me were not over yet.

DISCUSSION QUESTIONS

1. Which story was your favorite, and why?
2. Was there one story that effected you or stayed with you more than the others?
3. Did the Stepping-Stones symbolism help you?
4. Will you make different choices concerning your own healthcare now?
5. Have you made your family aware of your wishes around medical choices, funeral arrangements, and burial? Do you have an advance directive completed?
6. Are you less fearful of dying after reading *Stepping-Stones*? More fearful? And if so, in what aspects.
7. Are there things you have always wanted to do in your life that you have put off?
8. Do you feel that you are better prepared for dying?
9. Is there more you would like to learn about dying that wasn't in the book?

WHAT'S NEXT?

Are you wondering what lessons Wil had to offer Ellie after his death? Would you like to read more true stories about her patients and their walk along the Stepping-Stones pathway?

More Stepping-Stones is due out in 2021. This second book offers additional lessons, thought-provoking details, and insights from the experts—the dying patients.

Visit the author's website to add your name to the email list for updates about future book releases and her podcast.

https://eleanoratherton.com/

www.ingramcontent.com/pod-product-compliance
Lightning Source LLC
Chambersburg PA
CBHW020527080526
44583CB00013B/771